PENGUIN BOOKS

THE HAPPINESS PURPO

Edward de Bono was born in Malta, and after his initial education at St Edward's College, Malta, and the Royal University of Malta, where he obtained a degree in medicine, he proceeded as a Rhodes Scholar to Christ Church, Oxford, where he gained an honours degree in psychology and physiology and then a D.Phil. in medicine. He also holds a Ph.D. from Cambridge. He has had faculty appointments at the universities of Oxford, London, Cambridge and Harvard.

Dr de Bono runs the largest curriculum programme for the direct teaching of thinking in schools. Some countries, like Venezuela, have made it compulsory in all schools, and there is a growing use in Canada, the USA, China and the USSR. Dr de Bono's instruction in thinking has also been sought by such well-known corporations as NTT (Japan), Du Pont, Ericsson, United Technologies, American Standard, Exxon and Shell. His 'Six Hats' method is now used in many corporations, such as Prudential and IBM. He has also worked for governments, including the Government of California, on toxic-waste problems. He may be teaching senior executives of multinational corporations one day and nine-year-olds in a primary school the next.

Dr de Bono has been invited to address such meetings as the Institute of Institutional Investors, the Commonwealth Law Conference, the American Bar Association, the World Congress on Emergency and Disaster Medicine, the World Economic Forum (Davos) and the Society of Information Managers. In 1989 he chaired a meeting of Nobel Prize laureates in Seoul, Korea.

He is the founder and director of the Cognitive Research Trust (1969) and the Centre for the Study of Thinking, and the founder of SITO (Supranational Independent Thinking Organization), which was set up as a sort of intellectual Red Cross to provide additional and creative thinking on problems and issues. He has also set up a Task Force on Thinking in Washington.

Dr de Bono has been invited to lecture and work in forty-five countries. He has written over thirty books and there are translations available in twenty-four languages, including Chinese, Korean, Japanese, Russian, Arabic, Hebrew, Urdu, Bahasa and all major languages. He has made two television series, *De Bono's Course in Thinking* for the BBC and *The Greatest Thinkers* for WDR, Germany. He runs a newsletter that is published ten times a year and is the inventor of the classic L-Game, which is said to be the simplest real game ever invented. He is perhaps best known for originating the term 'lateral thinking', which now has an entry in the Oxford English Dictionary.

Other titles published by Penguin:

Atlas of Management Thinking
Children Solve Problems
Conflicts: A Better Way to Resolve Them
Edward de Bono's Masterthinker's Handbook
The Five-Day Course in Thinking
Future Positive
Handbook for the Positive Revolution
I Am Right You Are Wrong
Lateral Thinking
Lateral Thinking for Management
Letters to Thinkers
The Mechanism of Mind
Opportunities
Po: Beyond Yes and No
Practical Thinking
Six Thinking Hats
Teaching Thinking
The Use of Lateral Thinking
Wordpower

Dr Edward de Bono is world-renowned for his work in the area of creative thinking. His international seminars are invariably a sell-out. For further information please contact The McQuaig Group, 132 Rochester Ave., Toronto M4N IPI, Canada. Tel: (416) 488-0008.

Edward de Bono

The Happiness Purpose

Penguin Books

PENGUIN BOOKS

Published by the Penguin Group
Penguin Books Ltd, 27 Wrights Lane, London W8 5TZ, England
Penguin Books USA Inc., 375 Hudson Street, New York, New York 10014, USA
Penguin Books Australia Ltd, Ringwood, Victoria, Australia
Penguin Books Canada Ltd, 10 Alcorn Avenue, Toronto, Ontario, Canada M4V 3B2
Penguin Books (NZ) Ltd, 182–190 Wairau Road, Auckland 10, New Zealand

Penguin Books Ltd, Registered Offices: Harmondsworth, Middlesex, England

First published by Maurice Temple Smith Ltd 1977
Published in Pelican Books 1979
Reprinted in Penguin Books 1990
10 9 8 7 6 5 4 3 2

Printed in England by Clays Ltd, St Ives plc
Set in Linotype Juliana

Contents

The proposed religion is based on the belief that the legitimate purpose of life is happiness and the best foundation for happiness is self-importance.

The happiness purpose is to be achieved through the use of thinking and humour and dignity. The ideal of love is to be replaced by the more reliable practice of respect.

The new religion may be used as a framework or as a philosophy. It may be used as a way of living or a way of looking at things. The new religion may be used on its own or in conjunction with any other religion.

Unlike some others, the new religion focuses on the positive aspects of man's nature.

It may of course be that 'religion' is the wrong word.

The world may need a new religion simply because it intends to find one anyway

The old religions, including Marxism, were designed for a world of suffering. Buddhism sought to relieve the suffering by encouraging man to detach himself from his earthly self which was seen to be both the cause of the suffering and the sufferer. Christianity offered happiness in the next world and this salvation was to be gained by enduring the suffering in this one and using it to improve one's soul. Marxism suggested that man should look to the happiness of the state rather than his own and if the state seemed to require him to suffer then this was necessary for the happiness of the state. Today boredom has replaced suffering in the larger communities of the industrialized nations. Boredom includes confusion, lack of direction and a depression caused by the complexity of modern life. The relationship of the established religions to modern society will be discussed in the next section.

New religions are developing. They take two forms. Both forms are simple and direct but dangerous because they add nothing to the well-being of the world. The first form is the religion of opposition. Opposition has always been a most effective basis for a religion. Opposition offers a direction, a mission and a role. It offers self-importance and palpable achievement. It offers comradeship and organization. Above all it offers a definite value system against which to judge each action. The success of Christianity may have been due to the opposition that was forced upon it in the early days. The success of Judaism may have been due to the permanent opposition that has been its destiny. The success of Marxism is certainly due to its emphasis on the struggle against established capitalism. Indeed, so much emphasis was rightly placed on this opposition stage that little thought was given to what would be done if the opposition were too successful and removed what it opposed. There is always something to oppose, and those with a religious zeal can always find a cause to shape that zeal into a mission.

The second form of religion that is developing is that of self-abdication. Since the self is so boring and so much trouble it should be abandoned. This abandonment can itself take two forms. The first form is the handing over of the self to some outside power that is to run it for you. Let the stars run your self for you, or the party or your guru. The second form is that of ecstasy. By-pass the self and switch straight to the pure pleasure of ecstasy and mysticism. Drugs are an easy way of doing it and in time, perhaps, direct electronic stimulation of the brain.

Both the opposition and the self-abdication type of religion are anti-world in so far as they do not seek to make the world a better place or the individual a better individual. Many of the major religions had elements of both opposition and self-abdication. There was continual opposition to evil and especially to the earthly self with its greed and selfishness. There was also the element of self-abdication in mysticism, detachment and 'not me but God's will through me'.

Astrology requires no belief beyond the initial belief that the stars will run your life for you. Religions of opposition require no belief beyond the initial belief that there is a 'cause'. Once these initial beliefs have been acquired then there is an outside reference system that gives point and enjoyment to life. This outside reference system reduces confusion and makes decision easy. Man has always sought such a reference system outside of himself. Without such an outside reference system decisions are appallingly difficult and complex. The only solution is drift and moment-to-moment opportunism. In fact, any system requires a system outside of itself to act as a reference framework. This framework is

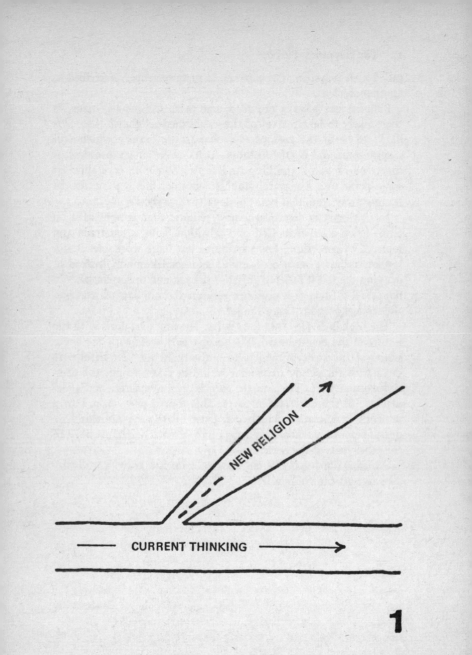

NEW RELIGION

CURRENT THINKING

1

called a *meta-system*. The purpose of meta-systems is described in another section.

Religion has always provided man with his meta-systems. Is there likely to be a revival of the established religions? If so, it is likely to be of the zealous and charismatic variety which will inspire some and alienate others. In its evolutionary progress, is the trend of man's thinking and feeling likely to crystallize at some point into a new religion? It may do. But it may also be leading away from that point of departure, as shown in Figure 1.

In this book is described a new religion that is not based on truth or on a belief in God and salvation. Love is discarded and replaced by something less wonderful but more workable. It is a low-key religion based on humour and good humour. Instead of denying the self it seeks to enhance the self and to emphasize *self-importance*. Because it does not rely on absolute truths it is possible to make a god of man's mind.

The book is divided into four parts. The first part deals with the *nature* of the new religion. The second part deals with the *application* of the basic principles to ordinary living. The third part deals with the *action* steps that would be taken to put the principles into effect. The fourth part is quite separate and independent of the other three parts. This fourth part deals with a network organization which can exist in its own right and requires from its members no acceptance of what is put forward in the other parts of the book.

· An essential feature of the new religion is a positive and constructive attitude of mind.

Part One
Nature

A religion that changes is dissipated and one that does not becomes unusable

Hinduism, Judaism and Buddhism are all over two thousand years old and Christianity almost that old. Islam is a later religion but still over a thousand years old. The only successful recent religion is Marxism which never set out to be a religion at all.

Is it possible that religions that were based on simple peasant communities can be of help to modern man living in a megalopolis of more than a million people? The direct answer is that they can, since they were based on an understanding of man's universal nature rather than his particular circumstances. Yet man was seen as man within himself and man within a small society. Man as an anonymous creature in a large urban society may be rather different. In a small community there is a community of belief which sustains doubters and puts social pressure on back-sliders. More important, there is a defined social system of behaviour and roles. There are expectations and rewards and penalties. In a way, any small community provides its own meta-system to guide behaviour. If this social meta-system derives its validity from a higher meta-system the effect is even stronger. And religion provided this higher meta-system. Teenage urban gangs and motor-cycle gangs are attempts to provide a community meta-system in large cities. Churches no longer have the same functional effect when you no longer know most of the people in the church. Today, instead of a religion moving down through a community to an individual it may need to move *up* through an individual to form a community.

Religions that are based on watertight belief systems do not suffer the atrophy that comes from continual adjustment to circumstance (since at each adjustment more is lost than can ever be gained). On the other hand, a watertight belief system carries with it the danger that one difficult belief or requirement may puncture the system for many. For example, the Catholic opposition to artificial forms of birth control may put many Catholics in a position of incomplete obedience. The dilemma is one that will come up again and again in this book: how far does one seek to hold the present position and how far to change it for a better one? The dilemma is simply that of stability and change. True evolution requires stable states *and* the possibility of change to a new stable state. Technological change, such as the development of the contraceptive pill, puts pressure on the change process. Technological changes require reactive changes from religions – for example, food taboos may prevent the full utilization of agricultural developments. Religions dislike reactive changes because this seems to open the way to change on demand – for example, with regard to abortion. And a religion that is run on a temporary consensus basis is but a political system. In short, a religion that changes on demand is no longer a meta-system that is outside the system. A religion that does not change may provide a meta-system that is no longer usable.

Traditionally religions have operated to protect man from himself and from his circumstances. It seemed that man had to be protected from his greedy, opportunist self that looked always for self-gratification and never at higher things. Enjoyment was a danger since it would lead at once to self-indulgence. Self-indulgence was bad for the person concerned (like a surfeit of ice-cream or alcohol) and also for society. Today man is somewhat more civilized and aware of his own nature. It should now be possible to allow enjoyment as a legitimate aim of existence and to encourage the self to develop patterns of enjoyment instead of abolishing a self which had any such inclinations.

Man is also able to change his circumstances in a way that was not possible two thousand years ago. For this reason the passive endurance of suffering is not the only mode to be encouraged. We can try to develop a positive and active outlook towards change. It is hardly possible to achieve happiness purely by changing circumstances. But change is possible and it can help. We may need to advocate both change and acceptance – instead of just acceptance.

Man is so much larger a part of the world than he used to be that his activities affect the survival of the entire planet. The world is no longer a vast universe in which man's camping made no difference. The world is a limited spaceship (to use Buckminster Fuller's term) with limited resources that require skilled management. Too many religions have urged man to look only to the next world and to save his soul rather than risk losing it by getting too involved in this world. Even today the drop-out dreams of a small country farm on which he is going to grow his own food while he forgets about the mad, frantic world outside. So who is going to get involved in running the world and its limited resources?

None of the defects outlined here implies real faults in the established religions. The defects arise from the very nature of a satisfactory religion. A religion deals with the nature of man, but its interpretation is effected by men living in particular circumstances. In time the interpretation takes over as the essence of the religion.

It can be said at this point that the particular view of truth that lies at the heart of the new religion makes it unnecessary to attack or criticize established religions or even to effect comparisons. Nor is the new religion an alternative: it can coexist *alongside* whatever belief system is in use. The new religion is like a table on which different foods may be served.

A meta-system provides a reason for doing something which does not lie within the immediate situation itself

A meta-system is a higher system outside the immediate system in which one happens to be operating. Perhaps the most striking example of the operation of a powerful meta-system is the way Christian martyrs went singing to their deaths in the Colosseum of Rome and elsewhere throughout the ages. Their meta-system of belief was so powerful that they were willing to give up life itself: the meta-system required that the operating system close down. A meta-system can make no higher demand. Not very different was the fervour with which the Janissaries and other soldiers of Islam hurled themselves into battle with a disregard for their personal safety. They knew that once a jehad or holy war had been declared, death in battle meant instant access to heaven.

In contrast to the Christian martyrs and the Islamic soldiers there is the opposite example of suicides or people who end their lives not through the operation of a meta-system but through the lack of one. From this must be exempted ritual suicide such as the Japanese hara-kiri which is another example of the operation of a powerful meta-system (though this time a social one and with no reward of heaven). I have known many people who have attempted suicide and several who have succeeded. If we leave aside the gesture type of suicide attempt there seem to be two mechanisms. One is a sort of temporary madness or rage and fury at life itself and especially at oneself. Though the end-point is different the process is probably not any different from any burst of destructive rage. The other mechanism is a sort of blankness or emptiness of the will to live. There seems to be nothing to look forward to and no point in life. The spirit appears to have died and so the body might as well follow it. It is sadly characteristic of depression that at the depth of depression it does not seem possible that anything can ever change or get better. It does not seem possible that there should ever be any enjoyment again in anything. No matter how many up and down swings a depressive may experience, in each down-swing he cannot believe that it will pass. The depressive exists from moment to moment. There is no meta-system of belief which allows him to get outside of himself and outside of the moment. Figure 2 shows how in the moments of depression a meta-system can provide the needed continuity and hope.

A meta-system is a device for reacting to something other than what is immediately under one's nose. Left to himself a child would eat poison berries (or medicines) because they were red and pretty. Human children would have difficulty in surviving if there were not the meta-system of parents who provide instruction that goes beyond the gratification of the moment. Because of his freedom of action a human child needs such an outside meta-system. A bird, however, avoids the poison berries because instinct has programmed him against them. Instinct provides an inbuilt meta-system – except that the bird probably does not feel attracted to the berries in the first place since he is not free to be attracted unless his instinct programme includes such attraction.

Gödel's theorem

To the delight of philosophers and mathematicians, Gödel showed that no system could prove the axioms on which it was based. For example, Euclid had to take for granted, and could never prove, the parallel-line axiom which stated that two parallel lines would never meet (on a *plane* surface because, of course, they do meet on a spherical surface). The axioms have to be provided by an outside system or meta-system.

Christianity was built on such axioms as the kingdom of God and universal love. These axioms were not developed from within the system but supplied by Jesus. Judaism was based on axioms supposedly handed by God to Moses directly. In the *Koran*, Muhammad provided the axioms from which the meta-system of Islam was to develop. Karl Marx in the *Communist Manifesto* and *Das Kapital* provided the axioms from which the religion of Marxism was to develop.

There might seem to be a big difference between meta-system axioms handed down personally by God, since God is the supreme meta-system, and those generated by a man such as Marx browsing through the British Museum Reading Room. Gödel's theorem, however, states that a system cannot *prove* its own axioms, not that it cannot produce them. The authority of the axioms handed down by God seem to prove their validity, but only if one already believes in the infallibility of God and in his personal transmission of the axioms. The basic Marxist axiom that the happiness of the state is more important than that of the individual is unprovable.

Since there is no way in which a system can prove the axioms on which the system is based it is open to anyone to set up a series of axioms and then to react to them as though they provided a meta-system. It is the belief that is *invested* in a meta-system that makes it work.

The nature of a self-organizing system will be discussed in a later section. It may be said that a self-organizing system comes about by chance and the laws of organization followed by the laws of evolution. Once the system is in being both processes can be much influenced by the development of meta-systems which, once created, become part of the evolutionary process. Self-organizing systems have no purpose except to exist and drift. That is why man has felt so strongly the need to receive or construct meta-systems.

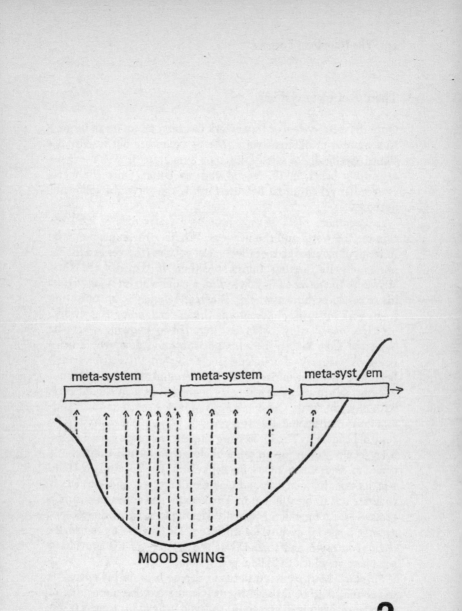

meta-system   meta-system   meta-system

MOOD SWING

2

The use of meta-systems

Once the meta-system or framework has been set up it can be used in a number of different ways. Meta-systems are not usually designed specifically to satisfy different human needs. Meta-systems arise from belief, myth, legend and revelation. Once the meta-system has gelled into a definite form it can serve the following purposes.

Explanation Meta-systems provide a framework of explanation for the world and the heavens. Whether the explanation be in terms of monster gods or theological entities it serves as a usable philosophy for linking things together. It provides the total answer to the never-ending 'why?' of a child who is trying to link his experiences into a whole. Whereas religion is an operating framework for man, philosophy is the understanding framework.

Origin and destiny Man is interested in knowing where he has come from mainly because he wants to know where he is going. A majority of religions (including primitive tribal cults) believe in ancestral spirits which hang around after death because it seems absurd that something as important as man should cease with physical death. Other religions provide heaven and hell both as a finite destiny and also as a reward and punishment system to control behaviour. The interesting thing is that once a destiny has been set up – even for no other reason than mental tidiness – it comes to exert an influence on behaviour. The ancestors come to watch over what one does and may require respect and sacrifices if they are not to breathe harm. The system also serves to ensure a proper respect for elders – usually lacking in systems that do not arrange a special destiny for ancestors. Origins are more usually clouded in myth and legend, but the mystery of life provides a solid base on which to build a god-system.

Purpose Man seems to need a purpose because his energy is too abundant to be satisfied by drift and a cow-like munching of experience. Man is so successful that too little of his time is taken up with eating and so more time is left for wondering about his purpose in the world. One of the prime functions of a meta-system is to give him a purpose even if it is only the teeny rebellious decisions of Existentialism.

Value The most important function of a meta-system is to provide a system for value reference. Animals tend to have values programmed into them by their instincts which dictate what they like, what they avoid, what they fight and what they do to each other. Man, in his multi-potential freedom, has no such programmes. But the price of freedom is decision. So man needs a meta-system to which he can refer in order to read off the values that are to affect his everyday life. In this way he retains both his freedom and a programme to make his value judgements for him. If he is a Christian then the Christian ethic and the road to salvation give him his values. If he is a Marxist then he has two value systems: the transition stage or struggle values while capitalism is being overthrown, and then the supremacy of the state value system.

Decision Decision is the application of values to action. Decision is easy when a powerful meta-system provides the values. The Christian martyrs and the Islamic soldiers were able to decide that the value of heaven and salvation was superior to that of betrayal of their faith and continuation of their lives. A terrorist has easy decisions to make if his meta-system tells him that all government forces are evil, just as the Nazi meta-system indicated that all Jews were of a sub-human value. It is in this area of simplifying decisions that meta-systems tend to be most powerful in action. And it is this practical power in action that gives meta-systems their appeal. People tend to take up a belief or meta-system because it reduces the *confusion* of their lives by making decision so much easier.

Judgement If decision is the application of values to action, then judgement is the application of values to reaction. Something happens and a person is called upon to react or give a judgement. He may of course be inclined to give a judgement even if none is really required of him. Social groups maintain their cohesiveness by a certain uniformity of approval or disapproval, shown most clearly in the English and Japanese concept of a gentleman. This uniformity of judgement, usually exercised as condemnation, is provided by the group's meta-system. Outsiders are kept outside and insiders are thrown out (or threatened with this) by reference to the values of the group meta-system.

Action When children are asked to draw machines (for sausage-making, hair-cutting, etc.) they equip them with buttons instead of mechanisms. You press one button for one effect and another button for another effect. This is a reflection of their world in which television sets, vacuum cleaners and motor cars are all activated by the right button. In primitive societies incantations or sacrifices to the right god had the same effect. A meta-system which put these gods into positions of operating power (like making it rain or making the crops grow) gave the users of the meta-system an apparent power of action based only on *knowledge* of the meta-system. Knowledge was power as it is today with science.

Achievement Man needs achievement almost more than anything else. Achievement gives him a tangible basis for self-approval and also for the approval of his fellows. Achievement is the currency of life. Without the direction, purpose and values given by a meta-system, achievement is difficult if not impossible. A child who is caught between the joy of building bricks into a house and the joy of knocking it down often finds that he is unable to build the house at all because of the conflict of achievement. Meta-systems not only clarify achievement directions but actually create achievement opportunities. The proselytizing and missionary opportunities offered by the Christian meta-system contributed very much to its success. The rituals and laws of Hinduism and Judaism offer tangible areas for achievement. There is as much achievement in carrying through a prescribed ritual as in opening up a new area. Meta-systems provide things to be done and ensure that these things are worth-while. Man is a busy animal but needs to feel that business is not an end in itself.

Simplicity Without a meta-system man would have to react directly to the many influences that press upon him from moment to moment. Today man is suffering from an immense information overload. He is bombarded with information: through education, through magazines and newspapers, through television, through advertising and through his fellows. There is a feeling that if some information is useful then one hundred times as much will be one hundred times as useful. In fact dilution and confusion occur and ultimately a sort of depressive apathy. A meta-system can be used to simplify the information input by providing a framework of priorities.

The hump effect One of the main purposes of religion has been to cope with the hump effect. Like the child and the poisonous red berries, man often finds himself in a position where his immediate self-interest is to act in a certain way: eat the red berries, steal a camera, tell a lie, seduce someone else's wife, etc. Religion provides the meta-system which tells him that in the long term such behaviour will not be in his best interests or, if this seems untrue, in the best interests of society as a whole. So the religious meta-system carries man past the temptation of immediate self-gratification in order to reward him with higher things. That is why the major religions have been so concerned with *attacking* self which is recognized as the source of selfishness and immediate gratification. Conversely a man may be required to do something which goes against his own nature in order to reap a long-term benefit. This might include such things as turning the other cheek to an enemy or giving money to the poor or studying at school when it is more fun to leave school. A meta-system is needed in order to make man do things which are not attractive at the moment. If we look at man's care for the attractions of the moment as 'now-care' and his care for the future as 'future-care', then a very important function of religious meta-systems has been to turn man's attention away from now-care to future-care. As will be seen, the meta-system outlined in this book is designed to change the balance back and to make man more conscious of now-care though still being concerned with future-care as well. With traditional meta-systems the balance was almost entirely in favour of future-care. The hump effect is so called because a person may have to climb over a hump before he can enjoy something. This effect is described more fully in a later section.

The community as a meta-system

Culture and religion are usually so closely intertwined that sep-aration is not possible. Like religion, culture can provide a meta-system (a reason for doing something which does not lie within the immediate situation itself). The operating meta-system for many people today is no longer the Christian religion but the Christian culture. Tradition and culture are also difficult to sep-arate, but tradition, like culture, provides a sort of meta-system.

A meta-system covering some parts of life can also be provided by a political creed or doctrine. Where this acquires the status of a religion-of-opposition then the meta-system comes to cover matters outside the political sphere as well.

In history the most powerful meta-system has been that pro-vided by the small community. The expectations of behaviour, rules and roles set up within a small community provide a power-ful meta-system. In part such a meta-system is derived from the background religious meta-system of the community, but the oper-ating meta-system also includes the *expectations* of the com-munity as such, including its individual social structure. Today when strong communities are being destroyed by ease of move-ment and communication, and mass cultural influences (adver-tising, records and television), the community meta-system disappears, carrying with it the religious meta-system. The com-munity meta-system was extremely effective, even if it did have one major fault. This major fault was the implicit axiom that 'being found out' was the key failing. This was not a matter of hypocrisy but practical operations: a community could survive so long as its rules were not openly flouted.

Internalized meta-systems

Most religions have tried to avoid the flaw in the community meta-system ('Do what you like but do not be found out') by creating internalized meta-systems based on the soul and conscience and an all-seeing God. The self-improvement of Buddhism puts the emphasis entirely on the internal self, and so cheating is impossible. Where adherence to a meta-system has had a definite external and visible form, like Christians going to church on Sundays, there is always the danger of hypocrisy inasmuch as the external application of the meta-system may suggest an internal application which is not there. As suggested earlier in this book, the need today is for an internalized meta-system that can *then* become externalized – and this is what the book is about.

Astrology

Astrology provides a nice example of a meta-system package which is easy to adopt. There are supposed to be specific personality types which are related to the birth signs. This gives both an element of individuality and also a reinforcement of belief, since personalities which fit the stereotypes reinforce the beliefs and those that do not are ignored. The stars control destiny and the future unfolding of events giving rise to a sort of fatalism. This is not a fatalism of despair but one of irresponsibility. Future-care is not worth bothering about since it cannot be altered. Moreover, there is the advantage that one can look into the future and see what is likely to happen (then using this as a framework-myth to be lived into much as a patient uses the psychoanalyst's interpretation as a framework-myth or mini-meta-system). The astrology meta-system is internalized in the sense that there can be no cheating since everything has already been determined by the stars. A person may, of course, conveniently pay attention to the stars when he wishes to and ignore them at other times – but that is no different from any meta-system. The interest in astrology indicates the strong yearning for a meta-system. As a meta-system astrology is anti-life and negative since it treats life no differently from the ocean tides. It is determinism in its most extreme form with human life affected by the stars much as iron filings are affected by a magnet. But this determinism indicates a need for a meta-system that can simplify life and reduce the burden of decision while at the same time enhancing the self.

Ping-pong ball

Without a meta-system an individual's life is like a ping-pong ball on a jet of water at the fair. It bobs about passively, totally dependent upon and trapped by the demands of the moment.

We can call it the happiness religion because it recognizes happiness as the legitimate purpose of man's existence

Some of the elements of the new meta-system described in this book are outlined here, and are dealt with in more detail in subsequent sections. Other elements which require more explanation are described elsewhere. So also are the practical operations which distinguish a religious meta-system from a purely philosophical one.

Happiness and enjoyment

Happiness and enjoyment are acknowledged as the *main purpose* of human life. Instead of being a sin as in the puritan ethic, enjoyment is regarded as one of the main routes to happiness. There are other routes involving activity and achievement. Happiness is regarded as something positive and not just the absence of pain and suffering. Happiness is also regarded as something which may have to be worked at and *achieved* rather than something which surfaces only occasionally like a porpoise in a quiet sea.

Positive aspects of man's nature

Religions have traditionally concentrated on the weak, greedy and selfish aspects of man's nature because man has been regarded as essentially sinful or at least too attached to earthly desire. The new meta-system acknowledges these aspects of man's nature in so far as they exist but puts the emphasis on the positive aspects. It is said that a state can generate any number of criminals it likes simply by creating laws that are likely to be broken. Similarly, religions have tended to test their adherents with laws and belief requirements that seemed designed to emphasize to man his sinful nature. In the Christian church in particular, St Augustine created the concept of original sin expressly to underline the role of the Church in leading man to salvation. There is some evidence that man grows to fill the nature that is ascribed to him. That is why the new meta-system emphasizes the positive and constructive aspects of his nature.

Life-enhancing

Life is something to be enjoyed and lived rather than a well of suffering to be endured on the way to better things. Life is not to be hurried through as a means to an end with our eyes on heaven rather than the flowers by the wayside. Life is to be enjoyed on its own terms. We can coin the term 'biophilia' meaning love of life. The new meta-system is definitely biophilic.

Involvement in the world

The new meta-system does not require a man to turn his back on the world. In its complexity and problems the world needs talented people to run it. For people with the right nature running the world is part of that activity which leads to involvement, achievement and fulfilment. Others are expected to make their contribution just as a lad is taught to make his own bed in the mornings. The new meta-system is world-accepting rather than world-rejecting. Total emphasis on the internal world of one's own self and self-awareness is not enough without a balance of external involvement.

Now-care and future-care

As part of the re-focusing of man's attention there is an emphasis on now-care: on the enjoyment of the moment. Future-care or investment in the future is also important but no longer has the exclusive emphasis it had in so many religions. The moment is to be enjoyed. The future is to be considered because such consideration will give in the future more now-moments to be enjoyed.

Self-enhancing

The new meta-system is definitely selfish. The self is the most important focus of attention. The meta-system encourages self-importance and self-valuation. The aim here is dignity which is the quiet worth a person gives to himself and as a result is accorded by society. Many religions such as Buddhism and Christianity are opposed to the earthy self that is involved in the world and capable of enjoying life. As will be shown later, they adopt different methods of subjugating this self and talk of the rapturous moment when man's soul detaches itself from his earthy self. In the new meta-system the aim is to integrate soul and self.

Humour

Humour in its most profound sense is the key *metaphysical* concept at the heart of the new meta-system. The focusing symbol (the biodic symbol), which will be described later, illustrates the implications of the humour process, especially as regards the behaviour of mind. In a less metaphysical sense the new meta-system is good-humoured and easy-going. This does imply a high degree of tolerance and individuality, but it does *not* imply drift, passivity, permissiveness or lack of direction.

Balance

As might be expected from the emphasis put on humour, balance is important. This is *not* the all-round balance of the perfect man but a conscious decision to operate at the most satisfactory point between extremes. It is not only a matter of balance between the ends of a spectrum, but a balance of attention when different things have to be considered: for example, a balance between now-care and future-care. Balance is one of the major areas for conscious effort.

A god of man's mind

The new meta-system makes a god of man's mind. It is man's mind that through the process of perception creates the world in which he lives. This is as surely *a creation* as the traditional god-created universe. Man's mind is the tool with which he re-creates the world to enhance his self and to obtain happiness. The emphasis is *not* on ecstasy whether induced by drug or mysticism but on the ordinary natural behaviour of mind as a patterning and re-patterning system. It is recognized that man's mind is immensely fallible.

New thinking system

In place of the traditional dialectics which sustained Greek and, later, Christian thought and provided (through Hegel) the basis for Marxism there is a new type of thinking based on positive evolution of ideas rather than improvement through polemic and clash. The emphasis shifts entirely from critical thinking to constructive thinking.

Truth

The new meta-system dispenses with absolute truths and hence with a belief system based on absolute truths. In place of absolute truth there is something called 'proto-truth' which is usable but improvable. Like humour, to which it is related, the switch from absolute truth to proto-truth is a key element in the new meta-system. Once absolute truth is discarded, a world of possibilities explodes in front of us. Arrogance and righteousness disappear and with them persecution. The switch from one proto-truth to a better one may be a matter for lateral thinking. Concepts are no longer *traps* but become stepping-stones to better concepts.

Respect

Respect replaces love as the operating basis of the system with regard to social intercourse. Love remains as a bonus and an ideal but no longer a working device. It is better to have a *practical working idiom* like respect than to have an ideal idiom like love which is fine in theory but rarely reached in practice. As with many other aspects, the emphasis is on usable and attainable goals, not on ultimate destinations and ideals. In this regard the new meta-system is low-key.

Activity and achievement

Being alive means being active. There is an emphasis on activity rather than on passive drift and time-filling. There are different sorts of activity, some of which are directed inwards (awareness and sensitivity) while some are directed outwards (altering the world). There is a balance between adjusting to circumstances and seeking to change them. There is a balance between improving oneself and improving the world. Achievement is recognized as one of the fundamental routes to happiness. This is not the achievement of competition and pressure but the simple achievement of setting out to do something and doing it.

Structure

The emphasis is on freedom and on plurality, but this is achieved through structure rather than through structureless mess. The structures are *liberating* structures that make it easier to do things rather than restricting structures that confine activity. *Focus* is an important part of the operating side of the meta-system.

System cheats

Because man is himself a system and because he lives in a social system the main condemnation of the new meta-system is directed at those who are able to abuse the system so long as everyone else is keeping it going: the smart-alec who is able to avoid paying his bus fare because everyone else is paying theirs. In the new meta-system the sins are *system sins*. Arrogance is another of these because it takes advantage of the proto-truth system.

Organization

The last part of this book describes a definite organization that bears the same relation to the meta-system described in the first part that water bears to a glass. You can drink water without ever using a glass. You can also use a glass even if you dislike water – there are other things to drink. There may, however, be a relationship of convenience between the two.

New words

From time to time it has been necessary to coin new words as I had to do when I invented the term 'lateral thinking'. This has been done with reluctance because new words are confusing. There are, however, concepts which cannot always be described with existing words without having to use a cumbersome phrase that is awkward to use and easy to forget. If the established word nearest in meaning is used then the special difference of the new concept may never emerge. For example, there is a fundamental difference between truth and proto-truth. There is also a fundamental difference between proto-truth and pragmatism.

The elements listed here are described in fuller detail in the appropriate section. A meta-system is only a framework. A framework cannot impose itself, but, like an idea, once it has come into existence it is there for anyone to use. The more effort and attention we invest in a meta-system the more valuable does it become. A meta-system is really only a *mirror* that reflects back effort as value.

The belief base of the new meta-system is the self-organizing principle as applied to the patterns of human perception

Not all religious meta-systems have a god basis. And those that do have such a basis do not necessarily treat God in the personalized way that Christians do. For many religions God is the organizing principle of the world, or the spirit of life, or self-knowledge of one's own being. But meta-systems that dictate types of behaviour and values tend to have a solid belief basis. The more difficult or unnatural the behaviour the stronger the belief base has to be. A Christian martyr really does have to believe in salvation and heaven. An Islamic soldier may have been conscripted anyway or be fighting as a job but to throw himself into battle with reckless abandon he will have to believe that death in a holy war means instant salvation. Buddhism does not have a god basis but there is a strong belief basis in the cycle of life and the need to free oneself from the continual cycle of birth and re-birth into a painful world. Religions which have not had a strong belief basis have tended to atrophy. The more sophisticated amongst the ancient Greeks did not seem to take their gods and goddesses seriously except as a basis for myth and poetry.

A religious meta-system runs the risk that if belief wilts then only ritual, habit and social pressure can keep the meta-system operating. Fortunately belief is an *emotion* rather than the result of intellectual activity. Astrology, like many ancient religions, relates its belief structure to something that can be seen and measured: the position and movement of the stars in the sky. But belief is still necessary to form any connection between this visible process and man's destiny. The same sort of belief jump was necessary to link the physical characteristics of a sheep's entrails to the destiny of a general about to go into battle.

Man has a hunger for belief because he has a hunger for order. Ordinary science and explanation are not able to satisfy this hunger and so belief has to create systems instead, just as a mother often has to invent explanations to satisfy the explanation hunger of a child. Once created, the belief system may take off on its own if it supplies other emotional needs as well – for example, hope or alleviation of suffering.

Like astrology, Marxism can point to something finite and measurable in the behaviour of an economy. The next step is still a matter of belief, since the preferring of state happiness to individual happiness is a matter of choice based on a belief in the role of the state. The Confucian system of ethics was based on a sense of the 'proper' functioning of society but did not seem to have a strong belief base.

God as creator

Most religious belief systems establish God as the creator, organizer and operator of the world. The world is his handicraft. He has to be appeased and also asked to do things which man cannot do for himself (like making it rain). Amongst God's other creations there is man. Because God has provided him with an origin it seems likely that there is also provision of a destiny. At any rate man created God enough in his own image to suppose that God would be interested in how man was doing. It was also socially useful to believe that God was interested in the behaviour of each individual, who was therefore obliged to obey God's laws as interpreted by his priests.

Darwin's theory of evolution was never proved in any way. It was just a theory and a speculation. But it did provide a plausible explanation to show how the different species could have evolved without each one having had to be created by God. The defenders of God's creation quite sensibly pointed out that there did have to be at least one original species, that the God-directed infusion of soul into the appropriately readied ape was what mattered, and that God himself must have designed the evolutionary process anyway. But the fuss was not about this. The fuss arose because many recognized that God had his origins in man's need for explanation and that if plausible explanations could be provided, then, even if the explanations were unproved, the *need* to believe in God was weakened. The crisis passed and it was realized that man's emotional need to believe in God and the relevant meta-system was more important than the intellectual need to believe in God purely as explanation.

Self-organizing systems

St Thomas Aquinas, in his monumental work that provided a thinking base for Christianity right up to this day, put forward five proofs of God's existence. One of them was based on 'causes'. Every effect had to have a cause and so on back until the first causer, who was himself uncaused, could be called God. It is natural to think that things will happen only if we make them happen. We tend to feel that anything complex has to be deliberately constructed or organized. But it need not be. There are self-organizing systems which operate by chance and yet produce an organized end-product which seems to have been put together deliberately.

You can make a chain of paper clips by attaching one to another in a deliberate fashion. You can also put a number of paper clips into a cocktail shaker and shake them up. At the end you will have a pile of separate paper clips quite unlike the chain that you had deliberately constructed. But if you now slightly open out each paper clip and put them back into the shaker for another bout of shaking you may get a surprise. At the end you may find that the clips have now *organized themselves* into a chain. The chain is nowhere near as neat as the one you made deliberately but nevertheless it is a chain of sorts – and quite distinct from a pile of separate paper clips. You have created a simple self-organizing system.

The basis of a self-organizing system is what we might call 'stickiness'. With the unopened paper clips one clip could as easily break free from another as come into contact with it. But with the slightly opened clips there was an element of stickiness. Once something had happened (two clips intertwining) it was much more difficult for it to unhappen – in other words, there was some *event stickiness*. As you continued shaking more events (connections) would happen and they would not unhappen until all the clips were fully occupied or at least not free to make further contacts.

It is suggested that life may have arisen by a somewhat similar process. Under certain conditions, such as those created by the electrical discharge of lightning, gases like ammonia and carbon dioxide can link up to form simple amino acids and these in turn can form protein and the elements of life. The appropriate gases have been detected in space. Like Darwin's idea, this provides a plausible explanation for the origin of life. It is also possible that, for inanimate matter, different forms of energy and fundamental particles interacted and self-organized to give the atoms and chemicals we know.

Once a basic self-organized system has come into existence then it can evolve and interact with other such systems to form larger systems. Evolution is a form of self-organization. A random mutation causes a gene change and the result provides the organism with a new feature. This new feature 'sticks' if the creatures carrying the feature are more successful at surviving and so pass on the gene to their offspring. It is also possible that the changes are not caused by random mutation but by spontaneous reorganizing of the gene material on a self-organizing basis.

As we shall see in another section, our perception of the world also operates on a self-organizing basis. Our brains provide a means for incoming experiences to organize themselves into definite patterns. These patterns then determine how we look at the world and with what concepts we think.

Society itself with its political and organizational structures also tends to progress in a self-organizing and evolutionary manner nourished by a soup of ideas and circumstances.

It is characteristic of self-organizing systems that they reach a plateau of stability which is held for a long time. Then, under suitable circumstances, the stable state may change to another stable state just as chemicals interact to produce new chemicals. With regard to the physical world of atoms and molecules, the plateaux last for billions and billions of years. With the self-organizing system of living organisms the time scale is shorter but measured in millions of years. With the self-organizing system of our minds the time scale may be measured in centuries. But technological change may have speeded this up so that it is measurable in decades rather than centuries. The same may apply to our social and political structures.

God and self-organizing systems

The principle of self-organization might seem to make God superfluous as a creator. Yet it could be argued that it was God who designed the system to be self-organizing. In any case, in many religions God is regarded not as a personalized entity but purely as *a principle of organization*. The Greeks paid a great deal of attention to mathematics because they saw something divine in its organizing principles. Pythagoras started a religion that was closely connected to numbers and geometry. Religions that refer to God as the principle of life may be said to refer to him as the principle of self-organization. For Hindus there would be nothing strange in regarding God as the principle of cosmic organization. One of St Thomas's five proofs of God's existence referred to him as the ultimate designer, and this is very close to the principle of design or organization.

Belief and the new meta-system

The new meta-system rests on a belief in the principle of self-organization and evolution – especially as applied to the perceptions of man. Principles of self-organization can be investigated mathematically and experimentally as can the principles of perception, so the belief is not a difficult one. Although the principles of self-organization do actually provide the basis for the meta-system, this is just as capable of operating from a different belief base (just as the Christian meta-system can operate from a base of divine revelation, historical scriptures, scholastic theology or pragmatic ethics).

A proto-truth is usable and believable – but only if you are prepared to change it for a better one

Truth is so central to human affairs that every religion and every philosophy has had to consider it before anything else. This is hardly surprising because, just as a navigator needs his map of the oceans, so we need a map of the world in which we have to live. Like a navigator we want this map to be as true and accurate as possible. A navigator with an incorrect map will never reach the destination he has chosen: he will arrive at the wrong place or end up on a reef. We want our explanations of the world to be true because that makes them usable. Science is a continual search for truth. It was our true understanding of the nature of bacterial disease that allowed us to conquer it. If we arrive at a true understanding of cancer we might be able to do the same for it. In matters of religion it is the truth of what we believe in that has given strength to the actions based on that belief. We feel that we can build if we have truth as a foundation – but without truth any building will crumble.

The need for absolute truth

Because we can understand falsity, lies and errors we are able to understand truth as the absence of these. Once we can understand truth then we can make that truth better and better until we arrive at absolute truth. Absolute truth is perfect and un-changeable. We need such absolute truth as the basis for our re-ligions and philosophies.

We imagine that we believe in what is truth, but more often we hold as true what we want to believe in. It is the strength of our beliefs that gives strength to the truth on which they are based. Faith is more likely to create the truth than truth is to create faith.

We need absolute truths to give us decisiveness for action. In science we have tended to accept truths as absolute, and when they turn out not to be absolute we just shrug and move on to the new truth which we again hold as absolute. There almost seems to be no point in using the adjective 'absolute' since we accept that truths should be absolutely true.

Types of absolute truth

There are many different varieties of absolute truth, and some are listed below.

Mathematical truth For the ancient Greek philosophers this was the perfection of truth. In a right-angled triangle Pythagoras demonstrated that the sum of the squares on the two short sides would always equal the square on the longest side. This would always hold true and could never be contradicted. It was in em-phasizing the continual search for this sort of truth which he held to underlie surface appearances that Plato set the trend for the truth-search that became the basis of philosophy and science in the Western world. What we tend to forget, however, is that mathematical truth only holds under a very *particular set of cir-cumstances* that are defined carefully in advance. For example, the Euclidean truth that the angles of a triangle always add up to two right-angles only holds on a plane surface and does not hold on the surface of a sphere where the angles add up to more than two right-angles. When we state the truth that two plus two equals four, we know that this only holds within the constructed system that we have set up. If three is obtained by adding one to two, and four is obtained by adding one to three, then it automatically follows that two plus two equals four. Mathematics is a constructed universe in which the truths are *implicit in our construction* or in our definition of the universe in which they hold.

Logical truth   Until quite recently philosophers spent a great deal of time with logical truths. On the whole these consisted in relating words in such a way that a new truth seemed to be obtained. It is now generally understood that these logical games were really word games and that nothing was proved that had not already been *accepted in the original definition* of the words used. The logical arguments only served to make clear what had been taken for granted. The classical syllogism was invented by Aristotle and re-packaged by St Thomas Aquinas. A classic example of the syllogism might run as follows: John is a man; all men are mortal; therefore John is mortal. The fact is that we only recognize John as a man because he has 'man-like' characteristics. So the syllogism is really saying: John is mortal and therefore John is mortal. So logical truths are similar to mathematical truths in that we set up a universe and then explore to see what is implicit in what we have done.

Scientific truth   Science is set on a continual search for the true laws of nature. Unlike mathematics or logic, science is not working in a constructed universe but in the *real* world. Science is the art of description and explanation. The truer the explanation the more useful it will be in allowing man to control his world. A description will seem true because it fits the available facts and then new facts are generated by experiment and a new truth is arrived at. Science is quite used to having its truths altered – even though they may have seemed absolute at the time. For example, the truth about the circulation of the blood in the human body was only arrived at a few hundred years ago. Scientific truth is rather like the truth that is used in law courts: the explanation seems to fit the facts best – if new evidence turns up we may have to find a new explanation that fits better.

Mystic truth   This is almost a pure experience of the sensation of truth. The mind of an individual is put in such a state that it experiences something which seems to be pure truth. This state can be arrived at by contemplation, by taking drugs or by prolonged starvation which has a chemical effect on the mind not unlike that of drugs. A mystic truth need bear no relation whatsoever to reality. It is almost as if the truth centre in the brain had been stimulated directly. We can electrically stimulate a part of the brain which can give a pure sensation of pleasure – even though nothing pleasurable has been experienced. Similarly mystic truth can give this end-result sensation without any real-world basis for it.

Revealed truth St Thomas Aquinas distinguished between truth that was arrived at by human reason and that which arrived direct from God as revelation. If we already believe in the authority of a source (such as God) then it follows that we must believe in what is offered as truth by that source.

Dogmatic truth Dogmatic truth is truth that we *create* as such. Dogmatic truth is truth that is decided upon and then set up as a truth. In order for it to be workable as truth there must be a general agreement to treat it as truth rather than to explore its basis. Dogmatic truth may at one time have had a basis in experience but the truth has acquired a momentum of its own, fuelled by the belief-emotion, and need no longer be based on experience. Dogmatic truth is not unlike logical and mathematical truth inasmuch as it sets up its own universe of perception. Dogmatic truth requires that we look at the world in a certain way – and when we do look at it in that way then our view supports the dogmatic truth. It is this circularity that gives dogmatic truth its strength. Freudian psychology offers a nice example of dogmatic truth. Sex is put forward as the basic human drive. If some action is recognizably sex-based then that confirms the hypothesis. If it is not recognizable as sex-based then the explanation is that a sublimation process is in operation and has disguised the sex-drive as something else. Either way the dogmatic truth is supported.

The process of truth

What happens to truths? We can consider several possible scenarios.

There are truths which cannot yet be shown to be wrong. Scientific truths of all sorts fall into this category. Further evidence or experiment or exploration may show an established idea to be quite incorrect. These temporary truths tend to be descriptive truths.

There are truths which can never be shown to be wrong. These are truths which hold in constructed universes and specially defined universes. They tend to be *circular* in nature in that if the universe is accepted the truth must be accepted as well. For example, if I construct a special universe in which 'a' equals 'b', and 'b' equals 'c', then in that universe 'a' will always equal 'c'. Mathematical, logical and dogmatic truths fall into this group. These are all special-universe truths.

There are truths which cannot be shown to be right or to be wrong. If you choose to believe that the planets do not move in set orbits because of the laws of gravity, but because each planet is supported by an angel that acts in that particular manner, then you are unlikely to be proved wrong even though you can never prove yourself right – except by reference to a special universe of belief. The problem is that one sufficient explanation *cannot exclude* other sufficient explanations. The adequacy of the gravity explanation does not disprove the accuracy of your angel explanation. All it can do is to make it unnecessary.

Proof and truth

The scientific tradition seeks to overcome the problem created by superfluous truths (truths which cannot be proved right or wrong and which seem superfluous to an established truth) by requiring proper proof of any truth. The attempt to extend this principle to all aspects of truth neglects the subjective nature of human experience. It also neglects the validity of circular truths. If I believe that a certain pill is going to do me good and it does me good then it is no use claiming that scientifically it only contained chalk. If I believe that suffering and deliberate starvation will get me to heaven then I have created a special universe in which the suffering and starvation do have a definite value.

The consequences of absolute truth

Religious meta-systems tend to be based on absolute truths. This means that the truths have to be defended at all costs. It also means that conflicting truths must be wrong. Righteousness and arrogance follow: 'I am right and you are wrong.' There often seems to be a duty to impose the truth on those who have not yet been able to see it for themselves. As a practical spin-off this duty of imposition strengthens belief in the truth that is being imposed. Persecution and intolerance tend to follow – but not necessarily, since there are many religions which jealously guard their own absolute truths but make no attempt to impose them on others.

The Greeks used absolute truth as a destination: something to be worked towards even if it could never be reached. This is the way a scientist uses truth. Christians have tended to use it as a way of life.

The main problem created by absolute truth is that it is perfect and unchangeable – and hence arrogant. Since any person or group of people is entitled to consider as absolute any temporary or dogmatic truth, this arrogance can lead to trouble. The arrogance of Marxism equals that of Christianity – and why should it not, since both are possessed of absolute truths?

Proto-truth

What would happen if we discarded the concept of absolute truth? What would happen if we threw out absolute truth from its central position in philosophy and in religious meta-systems?

We could replace absolute truth with temporary or contingent truths. In areas such as science this would only seem to be acknowledging what any proper scientist knows to be the position anyway. Karl Popper has suggested that the purpose of an hypothesis is not to be proved but to be disproved so that a better one can emerge. Scientific truths are temporary truths which may seem absolute at the time but are later replaced by others. Newton's truths seemed a perfect and absolute explanation until Einstein came along and provided a different explanation. In time Einstein's concepts will certainly be replaced by an even newer truth.

We can look at the evolution of truths in the same way as we can the evolution in any self-organizing system. There is a stable state which continues for some time. Then there is a period of change to a new stable state which again lasts for some time. This gives a series of plateaux as shown in Figure 3. All the time the truth is 'improving'.

We can call these plateaux or stable states 'proto-truths'. We can treat them as truths in all respects except one: a proto-truth is *always* held to be changeable and is never regarded as absolute. A proto-truth is only changed for a better proto-truth. There is a constant readiness for change but at the same time a willingness to use the proto-truth *as if it were absolute*. It is very important to realize that the rejection of absolute truths does *not* mean that no truth is possible and that we should not try to find any. On the contrary, it means that we can freely believe in and use truths because we no longer fear being *trapped by them*. We often reject absolute truths because we fear the consequences of accepting them. The same fear is not present with proto-truths.

Proto-truths satisfy the dilemma that has become more and

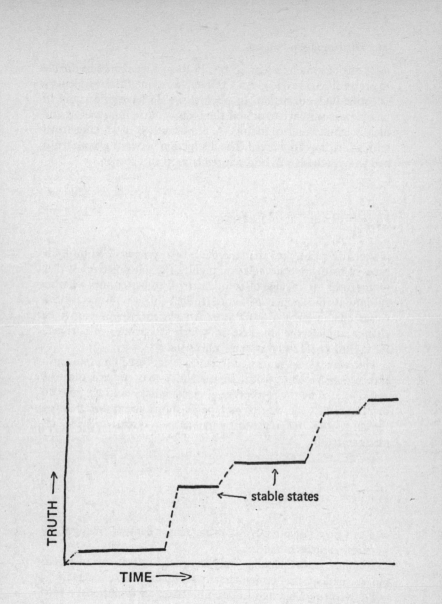

stable states

TRUTH →

TIME →

3

more obvious in our scientific age. In theory we should be unable to act until science had given a full explanation of the world and a scientific basis for action. In practice we do have to act and in many areas we have to act on the basis of little information and little scientific understanding. A proto-truth is a working truth with which we can proceed. The distinction between a proto-truth and an hypothesis will be discussed later in this section.

Proto-truths and absolute truths

It should now be clear that there are two systems of truth. Both types of truth are believable and usable. The sole difference is that proto-truths are capable of being changed to better ones whereas absolute truths are not. Absolute truths hold sway in special universes and in circular situations. An absolute truth cannot be changed unless the universe in which it operates is changed. Proto-truths hold sway in 'open' universes.

The meta-system suggested in this book is based on proto-truth rather than absolute truth. In particular it is realized that the world created by the perception of man's mind is entirely a world of proto-truth: one way of looking at things is capable of being replaced by a better way. Most religious meta-systems are based on absolute truth.

Practical varieties of truth

We can now put proto-truth in its proper context amongst the practical varieties of truth:

Absolute truth Obtains only in special universes and in circular situations; may be deliberately set up by belief or dogma.

Proto-truth Obtains in open universes; an evolutionary type of truth which is usable as truth in every way but which is capable of replacement and change.

Hypothesis A temporary arrangement of experience to be used as a framework for exploring that experience further.

Pragmatic truth Something which is held to be true because such a belief is useful.

Proto-truth and hypothesis

It is important to make a clear distinction between the two. In its essential meaning an hypothesis is a sort of guess which creates an explanation of events which can then be used to design experiments. Any hypothesis is a provocative tool of science. For example, I might have an hypothesis that certain species eat their young when upset in order to keep the population constant in an area. My hypothesis would suggest that in conditions of overcrowding there would be changes in the brain leading to production of chemicals that made an animal more easily irritable. Such animals would be easily upset and so would eat their offspring. Such an hypothesis would lead to a variety of experiments: measuring chemicals in the brain; using tranquillizers; comparing the provocation thresholds of animals from overcrowded areas with those of animals from less densely populated areas; observing other instances of irritation in overcrowded areas; etc. After thorough research there might be enough evidence to support a conclusion. This conclusion would become a proto-truth. The proto-truth could itself be used deliberately as an hypothesis by someone else who would confirm the proto-truth or replace it with a better one. The essential difference is a matter of use: a proto-truth is a conclusion (even if short-lived) whereas an hypothesis is a provocative experimental tool.

Proto-truth and pragmatism

This is another important distinction. Pragmatism was developed by the American philosopher William James who derived the idea from Charles Peirce, another American. Pragmatism holds that there is no truth except the 'cash-value' of an idea. In other words, a statement is true only if it makes a *practical* difference to life. This is generally interpreted to mean that a statement is true only if it is useful. At once huge dangers open up. The Nazis may have found it useful to consider the Jews as sub-human because this gave their followers a feeling of superiority which was important for the functioning of the Third Reich. The Catholic Inquisition may have felt that it was useful to burn apparent heretics because it kept others in line. Truth can usually be rationalized around actions which seem useful. A proto-truth does not have to be useful or even usable. It may make no difference to life at the moment. It is simply a truth which is acknowledged to be replaceable.

The consequences of proto-truth

Once absolute truth is replaced by proto-truth a number of possibilities at once explode into being.

Defence It is no longer necessary fiercely to defend the truths one holds, as is the case with absolute truths. A proto-truth does not have to be kept intact. It can be changed or replaced if an alternative is shown to be better. At once this replaces polemic, clash, debate and dialectic with a mutual *exploration* of the situation. Instead of two people each try.ng to prove the other wrong there can be an exploration of the situation and the proto-truths involved, with the intention of constructing a better proto-truth. This makes use of the process of 'exlectics' rather than dialectics (the process of exlectics is discussed later).

Persecution and intolerance Persecution no longer makes

sense. It is replaced by tolerance and a readiness to accept alternative proto-truths. Proto-truths do not have to be unique in the sense that absolute truths need to be unique. Proto-truths may indicate different stages in the evolutionary thinking of another person or group or different evolutionary pathways. Just as there are different competent animal species so there can be different competent proto-truths.

Man's mind The new meta-system suggests that we make a god of man's mind. In the past this was never possible because it was realized that man's mind is very liable to make mistakes and also to be deceived by illusions. Man's mind was rejected because it could not generate satisfactory absolute truths. But if we accept fallibility and proto-truths then we can accept that man's thoughts can evolve through one proto-truth to a better one. So long as we know that proto-truths are always replaceable by better ones, fallibility does not matter. At the same time we can use the positive, constructive aspects of man's mind.

The practical use of proto-truths

There can be personal proto-truths, group proto-truths and cultural proto-truths as well as more universal ones arrived at by consensus. Proto-truths are ways of looking at the world, and the experience-histories of different people will lead to different proto-truths. There may seem an obvious danger here that an individual or group may have arrived at a rather peculiar proto-truth which constitutes a danger to other people (like the Manson cult in the USA). If such a person or group is entitled to its own version of truth, does this not open the way to anarchy? The answer is that because a proto-truth is only a temporary truth it cannot be held with sufficient intensity to interfere with the rights or proto-truths of others. Subjective truths are valid so long as they are not objectively imposed on others. In any case a person or group who have considered their own version of truth as *absolute* are not going to be made more dangerous by being told that it is not absolute but only temporary. The trend would be towards reducing such dangers along with the reduction in arrogance and intolerance.

Like any other truth, a proto-truth should be free of deliberate error or deception. It should also be based on a full consideration of the situation, not just on a tiny part of it or a special point of view. The requirements for a proto-truth are no different from the requirements for truth as we now accept them – the only difference is the acknowledgement of the possibility of improvement or replacement.

The Buddhist meta-system insisted that the human mind can only perceive illusion, not reality. The mind has to be trained away from illusion until it is released into a state of contemplation of pure reality. The new meta-system insists that illusions are usable and workable and may be regarded as proto-truths. This does not mean that every illusion is a proto-truth but that some illusions may be regarded as proto-truths and others will still be regarded as illusions. The distinction is based on the application of the usual criteria of evidence, proof, fit and consensus.

The same distinction can be made between subjective proto-truths and objective proto-truths as is now made with truth. The only difference is that the arrogance of absolute truth is removed from both.

It may be suggested that if there is no such thing as absolute truth then it is better to dispense with the illusion of truth entirely. This attitude would mistake the functioning of a self-organizing and evolutionary system. Animals are 'definite' enough even though they may in time evolve into better animals. It is only because we are so used to considering truth as absolute that proto-truth seems worthless. In fact proto-truth is of more value than absolute truth because it is evolutionary. We can use proto-truth with confidence because we know that we are not going to be *trapped* by it. Proto-truth is not another word for doubt or indecision. On the contrary it makes for definiteness and decisiveness: we must use the proto-truth we have at the moment as we have to do in science. Without proto-truth life is a meaningless drift of confusion.

The essential point about a proto-truth is that we can use it and believe it – so long as we are prepared to improve or replace it with a better one.

A proto-truth may seem intangible in the way water is intangible. It cannot be handled and attacked because it is so fluid. But there is nothing intangible about the way water supports a boat. Just as a boat makes its way over water so we can live our lives supported by proto-truths that are fluid and changeable.

Man's mind creates the perceived world in which he has to live as surely as God created the external world

Most religions have firmly rejected the mind of man. This has been because his mind is seen to be subject to deceptions and illusions or else because his mind is seen to serve the earthy-greedy self that has to be suppressed before salvation can be achieved.

The new meta-system suggested in this book treats the mind of man as god. Traditional religions of all sorts are agreed that God created the universe. Whether this was done directly in six days as suggested in the book of Genesis, or whether God is the principle of life and organization as believed by the Hindus does not matter: the fact remains that God created the world and therefore we worship him as God. Man has to live in the world created by his mind. Through the process of perception the mind of man creates his world just as surely as God is credited with creating the physical world. If we regard God as the principle of organization and even as the principle of self-organization then the mind of man is the principle of organization that allows him to perceive the world and so create the internal world through which he is going to live. It is the *map-maker* who actually creates the world in which the navigator is going to navigate. This world may or may not correspond exactly to the real world. In the same way our minds create our worlds and these may or may not correspond to the real world, depending on the organizing characteristics and knowledge of our minds.

The mind of man has no inbuilt programme of instincts which

offers a ready-made map of the world. That is why the human infant requires years of self-education before it can cope with the world, whereas a new-born fawn can cope almost at once. The mind of a child has to create its own world through experience organized by perception into an internal world that is an ever-improving map of the external world. Education and second-hand experience are only devices to enrich the field in which this self-educating process happens.

A five year-old child refuses to drink his milk at breakfast. His mother explains that just as a car needs petrol to go, so the milk is his petrol and it will make him swim better in the pool. The child drinks the milk at once. Has the mother fooled the child? Not at all. The petrol–car relationship is a more accurate description of the milk than is the physical appearance of a glass of milk. The important point is that a change in the child's perception of the milk has made a definite difference to his behaviour. Jean Liedloff in her account of her visits to the Yequana tribe in South America tells how the tribesmen seemed to treat the irksome job of portaging a heavy dug-out canoe as fun whereas the Europeans made a great fuss about this tiresome chore. Again the perception of the situation changed the attitude and the behaviour. A group of thirty children aged between ten and twelve were doing the first lesson in a programme devised to teach thinking as a direct skill. The children were asked if it would be a good idea for each pupil to be given a weekly wage for going to school. Every one of the thirty children was delighted with the idea – they could buy more sweets and comics and have fun. The children were then asked to consider, quite deliberately, the plus and minus points arising from the suggestion (this exercise was the object of the lesson). They now looked at a broader picture and wondered where the money would come from; they suspected they would be no better off because parents would withhold pocket money and schools would probably raise charges; older boys might beat up the younger ones to take the money. Twenty-nine out of the thirty children had now completely changed their minds about the idea – simply through being given a direct strategy for broadening their perception of the situation.

Although traditional religions distrust the mind, they do rely on the ability of perception to create the internal world in which man is going to live. For example, a Christian's acceptance of suffering, and self-infliction of suffering, arises from a perception of the world that has been completely altered by Christian beliefs. The Buddhist is expected to develop a perception of the world in which his self belongs not to him but to nature. Man acts according to his perceptions. Religious meta-systems succeed by altering these perceptions. The new meta-system treats perception directly as being all-important: as the creative god of man's being.

Perception as a self-organizing system

The eye (or another sense organ) is only part of the perception process. It is the brain that does most of the work to organize the signals from the external world into recognizable patterns that have meaning. To be more exact, the brain simply provides a structure within which the incoming sensory signals *can organize themselves* into meaningful patterns. The nerves in the brain convert the sensory signals into a form that can self-organize itself into stable patterns. The brain is quite passive in this respect. It is not a matter of an ego choosing, sorting and organizing information. The information does its *own* organizing. The process is described in detail in my book, *The Mechanism of Mind*. The outline given below is necessarily brief.

Towel and gelatine systems

The difference between the two fundamental types of information system can be illustrated with a towel model and a gelatine model.

In the towel model an ordinary towel is spread on a flat surface such as a table. Alongside the towel there is a bowl of ink. From time to time a spoonful of ink is taken from the bowl and poured on to the towel. An ink-stain results. The towel corresponds to the receiving or memory surface that records the incoming information. The spoonful of ink represents the incoming information or experience. After a while the surface will bear a number of ink-stains, as shown in Figure 4. The ink stays where it was put and does not fade or alter in any way. Thus a good record is kept of all that has happened to the surface. If we wanted to use this stored information we should have to use a separate processor which would measure or relate the ink-stains in some way. This towel model is the classic view of a computer: perfect memory storage and then a separate processor. It is also the traditional view of the human mind: a memory storage system and then a thinking system.

The gelatine model is different. The receiving surface is not a towel but a wide shallow dish of gelatine (table jelly or jell-O). This time the bowl of ink is heated up. When a spoonful of hot ink is poured on to the surface it dissolves the gelatine. But the ink soon cools down and stops dissolving the gelatine. When the fluid (ink and melted gelatine) is poured off, a shallow depression is left as the record of what has been done to the surface. This depression corresponds to the ink-stain on the towel. A number of spoonfuls are poured on to the gelatine surface in exactly the same way as was done with the towel surface. But the effect is quite different. At the end instead of there being a number of separate depressions corresponding to the ink-stains on the towel, there is a channel eroded in the surface of the gelatine (Figure 5). What happens is that the second spoonful of hot ink tends to flow into the first depression. The third spoonful tends to flow into the second depression and then on to the first. In this way a channel is formed. Once a channel has formed the recorded information is now no longer separate: it is linked up. If we were to pour on some ink in the fourth-spoonful position it would flow along the channel and end up in the first-spoonful position. In other words, a *pattern* has been established so that the information is linked together. It is as if when we see a glass we know that it is suitable for drinking from, because the two things have been linked together.

The gelatine model simply offers an 'opportunity' for the incoming information to organize itself into patterns. In the section on self-organizing systems it was mentioned that 'stickiness' was a characteristic of such systems: if something happened it was less easy for it to unhappen. In the gelatine model the incoming information attaches itself or 'sticks' to preceding information to create a pattern. Further information will tend to flow along these established patterns, making them deeper, just as water flowing through a river makes it deeper.

The gelatine model and the brain

As explained in *The Mechanism of Mind*, the functional relationship between the gelatine model and the process of perception in the brain is quite close. Instead of gelatine there is a mass of interconnected nerves along which electrical excitation flows. The junctions between nerves are called synapses. Excitation will only spread across the synapse if the conditions are right. A sensory input to the brain should cause a spread of excitation over all the surface giving rise to a sort of epileptic fit. But the excitation is limited because each excited nerve feeds into a central pool as well as to its neighbour. From this central pool an *inhibiting* influence is fed back to prevent the excitation spreading across a synapse. This inhibitory influence is proportional to the total number of nerves that are in an excited state. There comes a time when the inhibitory influence is just great enough to prevent a further spread of excitation. This leads to a limited and single area of excitation rather like the single spoonful of ink. If a particular junction or synapse is easily bridged (because it has been bridged before) then excitation will tend to flow that way. In this way the area of excitation flows over the network much as the ink flows over the gelatine model. Patterns are also formed in the same way. Readers who find this explanation inadequate are urged to read the book referred to at the beginning of this sub-section.

What is important is not the detail of the mechanism but the

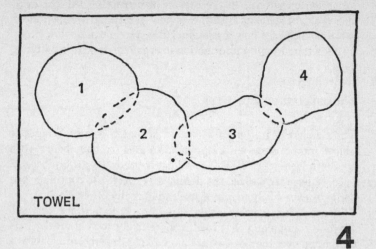

TOWEL

4

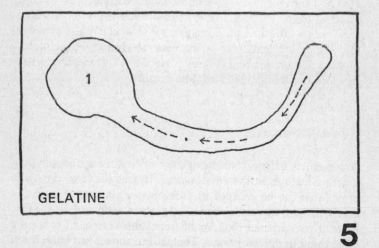

GELATINE

5

formation of patterns in the process of perception. All the available evidence suggests that this is how perception works. Indeed, it is difficult to see how a self-educating system could work except by allowing incoming information to organize itself into patterns.

The importance of patterns

The simplest definition of a pattern is that if one state tends to follow another state with a probability greater than chance, then a pattern is present. We call a wallpaper pattern a pattern because once we have recognized the design we expect it to continue: that design is more likely to follow itself than is any other.

The simplest way to show a pattern is as a track or road. Anyone going along that road is more likely to stay on the road than jump over the side (we are more likely to perceive a glass as a vessel for drinking than as a missile).

If the mind did not use patterns we should be unable to use language. Language is a code system in which a word indicates a whole pattern of meaning. The word simply identifies the right road and then our mind goes down that road to use the meaning attached to the word. If I hear or read the word 'glass' my mind explores the attached meaning-pattern at once. When you visually recognize a particular person your mind explores the pattern of what you know about him. A pattern is a sort of filing system in which one thing follows on from another.

Alternative patterns

A pattern is only a convenient way of linking up or grouping together features in the environment. Just as the same classroom of children can be grouped in a number of alternative ways (by age, by height, by colour of hair, by place of residence, by the first letter of the surname, etc.), so different minds can come to see the same thing in different ways. The pattern shown in Figure 6 can

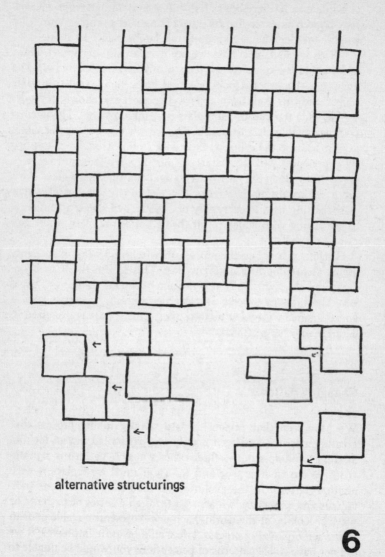

alternative structurings

6

be described in a number of different ways, all of which are right. A bottle may be described as half full of milk or half empty. A cow may be seen as a sacred animal by a Hindu, as a source of profit by a cattle-breeder, and as giving life to a landscape by an artist.

When we look at a glass we see it as a drinking vessel. How, then, could we come to use it as a missile in a bar brawl? The answer is that we are looking round for a 'hand-sized throwable object' and this leads us to a glass. The process is shown in Figure 7. The wide track leads from glass to drinking vessel. The narrow track leads from glass to missile. The narrow track cannot be taken at first because the other track is wide (more strongly established by experience). But if we start at 'missile' then it is quite easy to move down along the narrow track and end up with a glass. Puns are based on alternative tracks attached to the same words: 'vice' as something used in carpentry or as some evil habit; a 'golf-club' as something with which to hit the ball or as the place where golf can be played.

Humour is based on the process of *switching tracks*: of suddenly seeing something in a different way. This is also the basis of insight and creativity. It is also the aim of lateral thinking. That is why the humour process or pattern-switching process is such a key element in the new meta-system. This aspect is discussed in detail in another section.

Changing patterns

We have seen that perception is a self-organizing process that creates patterns. A pattern is only one particular way of looking at things and does not exclude other ways. A pattern is a proto-truth. We treat it as true and we use it until we replace it with another pattern. In the evolution of our thoughts, both as individuals and as society, we may go through a series of patterns or ways of looking at the world. Each one represents a stable plateau in the self-organizing process. Life would be quite impossible if we did not have stable patterns of perception: you would be unable to

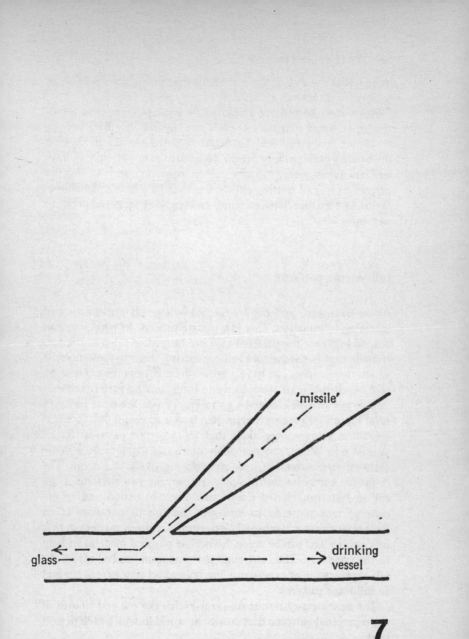

glass

drinking
vessel

'missile'

7

jump out of the way of a motor car in time unless your perception recognized its horn at once.

So we have to use our stable patterns of perception as proto-truths, realizing that they are not unique and also that they are capable of being replaced by better patterns. As usual, there is the balance problem: how far do we adjust to the patterns we have and how far do we try to replace them by better ones? An idea is a pattern or way of putting things together. We have to be able to maintain a balance between using and enjoying ideas and creating new ones.

Influencing patterns

As we have seen, patterns are formed by the self-organization of incoming information. This is a passive process. In what way can a mind *influence* the patterns that are formed? Although the pattern-forming is passive and self-organizing, the circumstances in which this happens can have a great effect. If you take a course on cooking then you are more likely to form cooking patterns than if you do not. If you choose to go to France you are more likely to form French language patterns than if you do not. If you focus on a problem you are more likely to develop further patterns than if you do not. When you put different things together by a deliberate effort of attention new patterns are likely to emerge. The deliberate use of lateral thinking can provoke new patterns. Logical analysis can clarify issues and direct attention and so encourage new patterns to emerge. The use of notation as in mathematics can conveniently exteriorize complex matters so that new perceptions can be made. Mental or physical models can help in the same way. Thus although patterns form passively from the self-organization of experience, man can affect that experience and so influence patterns.

The new meta-system is concerned with the use and change of the perceptual patterns that create the world in which each person lives.

Wisdom is a broad ability to look at the world and to look at one's looking

If a man is to be master of his own enjoyment of life he is going to have to do some thinking for himself unless he is content to let circumstances and other people do it for him. Bertrand Russell claimed that man was more frightened of thinking than of anything else. This is because many people believe that thinking involves having to solve a complicated mathematical or logical problem. But that is only a tiny part of thinking. Thinking is having to decide whether you want a chocolate ice-cream or a vanilla one. Thinking is telling a funny story. Thinking is going over in your mind a pleasant experience. Thinking is imagining what might happen next in the television thriller.

Thinking is the exploration and use of experience. That use includes enjoyment, problem solving and the setting of objectives. Thinking is like moving your finger over your own, personal, internal map of the world. The roads are the patterns created by perception. Some roads are more clearly marked than others and there may be areas with too few roads.

Purpose of thinking

Apart from direct enjoyment the purpose of thinking is to adjust oneself to the circumstances or to adjust the circumstances to oneself. Thinking involves active planning as well as passive contemplation. Thinking is like using a telescope or a microscope or a sketch-pad or a screwdriver. Happiness is a problem that is solved by developing an understanding of the world and of oneself, and then making use of that understanding in a practical manner.

Misconceptions about thinking

It is often mistakenly supposed that thinking requires a high IQ. This is not the case. Children with relatively low IQs (about 80) can still be effective thinkers. When people are dealing with their own experience they can be much better thinkers than when they are required to absorb new experience before they can start thinking.

People with high IQs are not necessarily good thinkers. In fact the possession of a high IQ can often be counter-productive. Many highly intelligent people are poor thinkers because they can never allow themselves to be wrong. They often take up an instant judgement position on a subject and then use their thinking *to support* that position rather than to explore the subject area before making a judgement. The more effective they are in support of their instant judgement the less inclined will they be to change this. The result is clever argument but ineffective thinking.

There is a very dangerous misconception that has been encouraged by education, and this concerns the use of the critical intelligence. Education has fostered the notion that the critical intelligence is the highest use of the mind. This notion arises from the days when education was controlled by the Church and it was necessary to put a high emphasis on critical skills since it was the criticism of heresies that would have to preserve the integrity of the Church. Criticism is a relatively easy form of intellectual achievement and much used by mediocre minds who are unable to be creative or constructive. You cannot grow a garden just by pruning: there has to be some planting and fostering of plants as well. We are apt to dismiss an idea because 10 per cent o. be in error, ignoring the 90 per cent that is worth-while. meta-system suggested in this book is much in favour of the pos. tive and constructive attitudes of thinking rather than the nega- tive destructive ones.

Many people open a learned book on philosophy and find that they can understand very little. They ascribe this to their own poor level of education or thinking. This is an unfortunate mis- take. The writer of the learned book on philosophy would, him- self, have been just as lost had he opened a book on electronics or polymer chemistry. Each specialized field of knowledge has its own concepts and its own jargon, and there is no shame in not knowing the jargon of all possible fields. It is rather up to the writer to communicate if that is the purpose of his book. Many learned people are experts in their own field because the depth of their focused knowledge does much of the thinking for them. Out- side their own field such people may be rather poor thinkers.

Intellectualism has deservedly got itself a bad reputation. It is possible to play logical word games in which one concept gener- ates another in a sort of virtuoso ballet of ideas. But it does not add up to anything except an amusing game played with the mind. Intellectualism is like a steamer with its propeller out of the water and churning the air: there is much happening but not much pro- gress. Thinking is definitely not reserved for intellectuals.

Scholarship is too often the triumph of form over content. A small and usually unimportant area is explored in great depth and detail. Larger and more important areas which cannot be treated in the same way are ignored. The emphasis which universities have placed on scholarship has contributed very much to their losing their once central role in the thinking of society.

Traditionally thinking has been put in terms of debate, clashes and polemics. This has arisen from our dependence on dialectics as the only form of developmental thinking. The dialectic process tends to be negative (extremely so when converted into action) and can be replaced by a more positive process that is part of the new meta-system and is described in a subsequent section. This new process of 'exlectics' seeks to draw out and improve what is good in an idea rather than to attack what is bad.

Because philosophers have largely been involved in word games or mathematical games, logic has come to assume a dominant position in thinking. In practice, when we are thinking about the real world rather than some artificially constructed world of words or numbers, perception is very much more important than logic. Most thinking is a matter of dealing with perceptions. Only a small part of thinking requires special logical manipulations. The insistence on logic has a dangerous spin-off: we assume that if an argument is free of logical error it must be valid. This is nonsense. Bad logic does make for bad thinking but good logic does not ensure good thinking unless the perceptions on which it is based are sound. We would do well to pay much more attention to perception (the way we see the world) than to intricate logical skills. The same thing applies to mathematics: we often pay all the attention to the correct manipulation of the symbols and none to the *initial translation* of the world into symbols.

Ignorance and information

No one can know everything. Thinking is usually based on incomplete information. It is sensible to try to get as much relevant information as possible, but impractical to expect to get enough information to do your thinking for you on every occasion. Thinking often involves guessing and speculation. It is an impractical habit, fostered by education, to refuse to think unless information is complete.

There are four different types of ignorance:

not having the information in the first place;

having the information but not using it because of inadequate scanning of experience;

having the information but putting it together incorrectly;

an arrogance which refuses to look beyond an apparently satisfactory solution based on only part of the situation.

The arrogance type of ignorance is the most culpable, the most dangerous and the most common.

Beauty and feeling

There is a notion that there is a divide between thinking on one hand and beauty and feeling on the other. It is sometimes believed that thinking destroys spontaneous emotional response and also kills beauty by analysis. It is imagined that the thinking person stands in front of a painting and instead of appreciating its beauty and responding with an emotion, analyses the style of the painter. This is a silly misconception fostered by those who equate thinking with intellectual games. The appreciation of beauty and feeling itself are types of thinking. The only difference is that they are not carried out with words or fixed concepts. To be able to feel about something is as important as, or even more important than, being able to think about it. But feeling should not exclude other forms of thinking since each can enhance the other. The new meta-system in no way suggests that everything has to be reduced to intellectual formulas. Thinking, in the ordinary sense of the word, is only a tool of feeling. The tool is used to create those situations in which enjoyment and happiness can best be felt.

There is a classical story of the centipede that was proceeding quite comfortably until someone asked it which leg followed which. The result was that the centipede became unable to proceed further as it lay distracted in the ditch wondering which leg came before which. There are those who feel that thinking will destroy their ability to feel or appreciate in an unintellectual way. Again it must be stressed that there is a big difference between thinking and intellectual analysis. Thinking enlarges the area in which feeling can take place and generates more opportunities for feeling: there is no antagonism between the two. A man who cooks brilliantly by 'instinct' is not made to follow an instruction book but benefits from being brought into contact with new ingredients to which he can apply his skill.

Mistakes

No one makes mistakes on purpose, but mistakes do get made. The human mind is fallible and it is ridiculous to suppose otherwise. Once this is realized, then thinking can be combined with the sort of humility that is described in the section on humour. It is because the new meta-system replaces truth with proto-truth that people can be allowed to think for themselves. Unless a person is capable of making mistakes then he is not capable of thinking. The mistake does not matter. What does matter is the attachment of arrogance to a mistake on the basis that no mistake could ever have been made. A person gains a great deal from a mistake and even more from an admitted mistake. He gains a new way of looking at things.

The ego and thinking

Thinking is too often regarded as an extension of the ego. Clever children in school base their egos on being clever and on being right all the time. They dislike group work because they cannot then show the rest of the class where the good idea originated. When the ego and thinking are treated as the same thing there is a reluctance to be wrong and a need to defend a point of view rather than to explore the situation. A person should be able to treat his thinking much as a tennis player treats his strokes: he should be able to walk off the court complaining that his backhand was not working very well on that occasion or that it required more practice.

The new meta-system is very much in favour of the self, but a self that is based on a proper sense of dignity, not on an inflated ego. A person who dare not admit he is wrong inflates his ego but weakens his self.

Unsolved problems

There will always be problems that cannot be solved. No thinker should pretend that he can solve all problems. Sometimes a problem is not solvable because it is posed in a self-contradictory manner which makes solution impossible. Here, attention to the problem is more important than attention to the answer. Other problems may have a solution which cannot yet be found by a particular thinker or by any thinker. There is nothing wrong with defining unsolved problems and coming back to them whenever one wishes. This should be done in a relaxed manner and not with a sense of anguish or frustration. The world will not be saved by the solution of a tantalizing problem. Such problems are best treated as friends or 'pets'.

Wisdom and cleverness

It must have become obvious in this section that the new meta-system is against cleverness and in favour of *wisdom*. Cleverness is a sort of intellectual games-playing which is enjoyable for those who enjoy it but not necessary for everyone (any more than a liking for fishing). Wisdom is a broad ability to look at the world and to look at one's looking. Wisdom is based on robust common-sense and humility – not on winning arguments.

Whereas dialectics seek to batter an idea into a better one, exlectics seek to build it into a better one

Marxism claims to be based on dialectical materialism. The dialectic process assumes that in time everything breeds its opposite. This opposite splits off and there is then a clash between the two. From this clash arises something new or a new idea. In formal terms a thesis breeds its antithesis and then thesis and antithesis clash and from this arises a synthesis. So capitalism gives rise to anti-capitalism and from the struggle between the two there arises the utopia of Marxism. The dialectic process was much considered by the German philosopher Hegel who became a strong influence on thinkers and doers of the nineteenth century. There was, however, nothing new in dialectics. The Greeks, and Socrates in particular, had based their discourse on the dialectic process, and the theologians and churchmen of the Middle Ages had done likewise. It seems a convenient way in which to work from one idea towards a better one. The evolution of better ideas is based on clash and struggle, rather as Darwin assumed the survival of the best-fitted species was based.

The danger with dialectics is that the negative and destructive elements too easily become dominant. *Negativity* becomes an end in itself. The best brains become involved only in negative criticism and consider this a sufficient endeavour. Destruction becomes an end in itself. Destruction and opposition provide sufficient direction to become the basis of another religion-of-opposition as described in an earlier section. Marx and Lenin were quite conscious of this and placed their full emphasis on the 'struggle' of the transition stage during which capitalism was to be destroyed. They were right to do this because this is what has given Marxism its practical fervour – just as trade unions have been most effective when in opposition.

We recognize the same dialectic process in politics in a democratic country with the added absurdity that an opposition feels duty bound to disagree with whatever the government proposes even if it makes sense.

The emphasis on opposition and clash rests on the assumption that the system is robust enough to *somehow* produce something new and better. But a system can only do this if it has derived a considerable momentum from somewhere. For example, the Catholic Church thrived on the opposition that caused it to tighten up both its doctrines and administration. But this easy assumption of a positive, constructive force, somewhere, may be mistaken. Where Marxism has succeeded in its anti-capitalist struggle the new utopia is nothing like as splendid as was the struggle stage.

So the major weakness of the dialectic method is the concentration on criticism and destruction on the assumption that 'somewhere' there is a constructive element.

Exlectics and dialectics

With the new process of exlectics suggested in the new meta-system the emphasis is on the positive, constructive aspects of the evolution of new ideas instead of on the negative clash aspects. In Darwin's evolutionary model the emphasis has shifted from the struggle-for-survival stage to the mutation stage. 'How do we change an idea into a better one?', instead of 'How do we batter an idea into a better one?' It is a matter of building on ideas, improving them and perhaps changing them rather than criticizing them. The exlectic process recognizes that construction will be slow to happen unless someone sets out deliberately to be constructive. It is not suggested that negatively minded people are incapable of being constructive but that they need to be pointed in a constructive direction.

The process of exlectics

The process is illustrated in Figure 8. The first stage is the exploration stage. This is a cooperative exploration with both parties exploring the situation or idea. Together they construct a sort of map. This map will indicate their points of agreement and disagreement. Disagreement may be based on fact, on interpretation and on different value systems. There will be agreement on some positive points and agreement on some negative points. There will be disagreement on some points which one side holds to be positive and the other to be negative.

The second stage is to extract a key-point from the situation. This key-point is chosen because it is crucial. It may be a point of agreement or of disagreement.

The third stage involves the 're-clothing' of the key-point. This can mean adding to it elements from the old situation, or new ones. The new ones may have to be created or borrowed from other situations. Only points on which there is an agreed positive attitude should be added. If the total idea ends up by being incomplete and unworkable then a deliberate effort is made to complete it or the whole process starts again with a fresh key-point being chosen.

At this third stage there is an alternative route. Instead of the key-point being 're-clothed' it can be changed deliberately to a new concept by the application of lateral thinking. In practice this can mean a cooperative generation of new concepts until both sides agree that they have one with which they can work in a constructive manner. The new concept would then have to be clothed as described above.

The fourth stage is the modification and development of the new idea to make it workable.

In formal terms the extracted key-point may be called the 'ex-

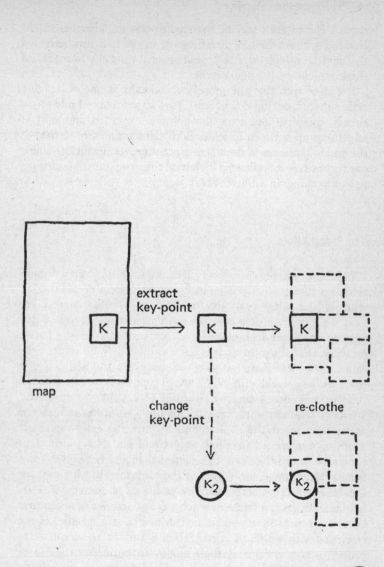

extract
key-point

map

change
key-point

re-clothe

8

thesis'. The exthesis may be changed to give an 'alterthesis'. The clothing of the exthesis or alterthesis gives rise to a 'neothesis' and the final acceptable idea is a 'proto-thesis'. But the formality of these expressions is unimportant.

It can be seen that the process of exlectics is one of *building* rather than knocking down. Since it is impossible to build on an already complete idea some key-point is extracted and used as something upon which to build. Both sides are now concerned in the building process. If the starting-point proves unsuitable a new one is chosen or it is changed by lateral thinking (moving sideways to look at things in a different way.)

The lump effect

Words and concepts cover many meanings. Quite often a dispute arises because one party is focusing on one aspect of the concept whereas the other party is focusing on another aspect. For example, the expression 'cow-like contentment' seems to be a derogatory one if we look on cows as being stupid, unimaginative creatures that allow themselves to be exploited. Who wants to be called a cow? But if we focus on the simplicity and harmony of a cow's life in a world with which it can cope then we can see some positive and indeed enviable features of cow-like contentment. Similarly with the word 'profit'. This lump word can be attacked as meaning greed and exploitation because the early capitalists were only interested in what they could get away with. This cannot be denied. Nor can it be denied that profits do often come from exploitation of the worker or the consumer. But if we escape the lump effect we can look on profits as a source for a re-investment that can create new jobs, as a source for new ventures that may benefit new workers or consumers, as a measure of the efficiency with which an organization is run, as an incentive for people to save and invest their money in businesses capable of raising the standard of living. All this is also correct. The dialectic process would insist on a clash between the two opposing points of view. The exlectic process might pick out the efficiency measure as a key-point and then in re-clothing it try to avoid the possibilities of greed and exploitation. The attitude is one of building on the good points and leaving the bad ones behind – instead of attacking the whole idea on account of the bad points. If it proves impossible to build on any of the good points then an attempt is made to develop a new concept: for example, in the case of 'profits' the new concept might involve reward for the investor based on the number of livelihoods he supports.

Changing ideas

An idea is an organization of features just as a pattern is an organization of features to give a perception. It is quite likely that the features can be re-grouped or re-structured in a different and better way. It is possible that adding some features or dropping others can lead to a better idea. It is possible that the change of a crucial feature can lead to a totally new idea. All this can be done by a process of positive reconstruction supplemented by lateral thinking. The critical and negative approach to new ideas is by no means the only method we have traditionally assumed it to be.

The new meta-system, in putting the emphasis on positive aspects, would seek to develop the idiom of exlectics in place of dialectics. The change-over may not be easy for those who can only think in terms of dialectics and clash.

It has always surprised me how little attention philosophers have paid to humour since it is a more important process of mind than is reason

The fundamental importance of humour in the new meta-system suggested in this book was hinted at in an earlier section. Just as most other religious meta-systems are based on belief, so this new meta-system is based on humour. In this respect humour is regarded in two different ways that are distinct and yet come together in the end. The first way is as an attitude to life. The second way is as a key process in perception. We can now look in a general way at the reasons behind the elevation of humour to a position usually reserved for more solemn matters.

Humour is positive and life-enhancing. The purpose of humour is enjoyment and happiness. This is very much the idiom of the new meta-system.

Humour is anti-solemnity. In place of fervour and intensity the new meta-system would place the liveliness of humour and its relaxation.

Humour is anti-arrogance. Humour is for tolerance and humility. You listen to someone else's story and he will listen to yours. Arrogance is a fundamental 'sin' in the new meta-system. Humour offers a proto-truth for a very brief instant. We accept humour for what it is.

Humour is accessible. You do not have to be a genius or a saint to have a sense of humour.

Humour arises directly from that process of perception which allows the mind to switch over and *look at something in a completely new way.*

Humour and perception

Perception is a pattern-making process, as we have seen in a previous section. The mind would be trapped for ever by its initial patterns unless it had the ability suddenly to switch over and see things in a different way. This is the basis of insight, creativity, learning and progress. It is the aim of the techniques of lateral thinking. This pattern-switching ability is vital to a patterning system which simply could not work without it. And humour is the most direct and obvious expression of this pattern-switching ability. We suddenly see something in a new way, as explained in the section on the biodic symbol, and we laugh. Because humour is so enjoyable and so easy and so apparently trivial we tend to overlook just how *fundamental* a process it is to the human mind. It has always surprised me how little attention philosophers have paid to humour since it is a more significant process of mind than is reason. Reason can only sort out perceptions, but the humour process is involved in changing them.

Because humour is the outward expression of this pattern-switching process it symbolizes such things as possibility, hope, change, creativeness, new ways of looking at things, evolution. Humour means that we can use our proto-truths knowing that we will eventually replace them by better ones.

Negative aspect of humour

There is a minor negative aspect of humour that perhaps ought to be considered. Because it is possible to laugh or sneer at everything it might seem that nothing is ever worth doing and the only solution is to drift along without effort or activity. This attitude to humour is similar to the negative and critical attitude of mind that has been discussed in earlier sections. The sneer is false humour. The true attitude is the deliberate putting on of fancy dress and enjoying it, knowing that it may be ridiculous if you choose to regard it as such – but not minding.

The biodic symbol illustrates the possibility of switching from one way of looking at something to another which has been present all along

The biodic symbol bears the same relationship to the new meta-system as the cross bears to Christianity. The symbol is shown in Figure 9. It shows two roads: a main track and a side track that leads off the main track. The junction of the side track with the main track is narrow although the side track later opens out to a greater width. The word 'biodos' comes from the Greek word for road, *hodos*. From *bi-hodos* we get 'biodos' and the biodic symbol. Biodos and the biodic symbol can be used interchangeably, but at first it is probably best to refer to the 'biodic symbol' since 'biodos' by itself will not especially refer to a symbol.

What the biodic symbol means

The symbol refers directly to the tracks or roads that represent the patterns formed by the mind in the process of perception as described in an earlier section. The main track refers to the main pattern. The side track is another pattern. The mind moves along the main track and *does not even notice* the side track because this is obscured by the dominance of the main track. This is a very important point because in a patterning system the flow of attention is passive and must as surely follow the main track as water will flow from a higher to a lower level. *There is no question of there being a choice between the two tracks.* The second track is normally quite invisible even though it is present.

If, however (Figure 10), attention starts at a different point, the side track may be used to enter the main track. So under normal circumstances the main track may not be left by means of the side track but can be entered from the side track: a sort of pattern-valve.

Sequence of experience

Patterns are set up by a particular sequence of experiences just as a particular sequence of spoonfuls on the gelatine surface set up a track. A different sequence of experiences may set up a different pattern or track. This process is illustrated in Figure 11, which shows a series of shapes that are presented in differing sequences. At each stage the object is to arrange the pieces to give a simple geometric shape such as a square or rectangle. It may be seen that one sequence may lead to an ultimately successful arrangement and another might not. In the same way once a pattern has begun to be formed by a particular sequence of experience it continues to build upon this sequence. The importance of this in relation to the biodic symbol is that initial commitment to one track may mean commitment to a particular track and the inability to use, or even notice, an alternative track. This is why a way of looking at things which may seem accurate and unique may in fact be only one among many possible perceptions.

Humour and the biodic symbol

In humour a particular sequence is set up to lead the mind along one main track. At the crucial moment a word or gesture indicates that there is an alternative track to which the mind at once

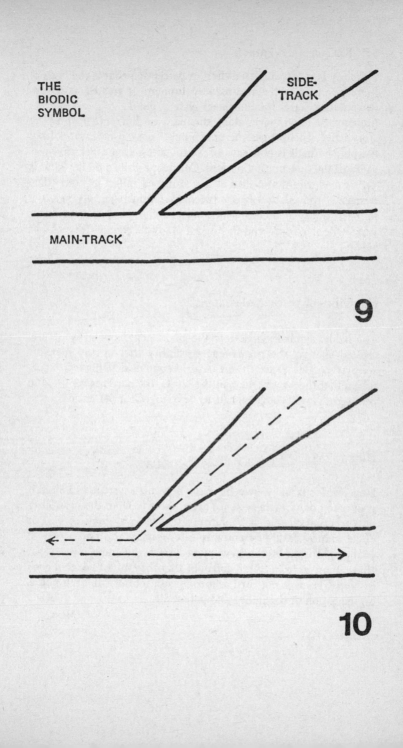

THE
BIODIC
SYMBOL

SIDE-
TRACK

MAIN-TRACK

9

10

switches. It is this sudden switch in perception that is the basis of humour and also the reason why humour is treated as a fundamental aspect of the new meta-system. Figure 12 shows how in humour the mind moves along the main track as intended by the story-teller. Then comes the punch-line. Looking backwards from the punch-line it is now easy to see the alternative track that was there all the time but not noticed. Consider a child's riddle: what is yellow and white and flies at five hundred miles an hour? The answer is the pilot's egg sandwich in a Jumbo jet. At first the mind naturally assumes that the object is flying on its own. But it is not (the side track) and this is just plausible enough for a child's riddle.

Possibility of perceptual change

The biodic symbol symbolizes the permanent possibility of perceptual change, the permanent possibility that at any moment we may be able to see things in a different way. This is a recognition that the way we look at the world, the patterns we use, the proto-truths we believe in, can all be changed for better ones.

Hope

Hope, which is a key element of the new meta-system, as indeed it is of many older meta-systems, arises directly from the possibility of perceptual change. It is not only that we may come to see our circumstances in a different way but we may also find a way of changing them. In the new meta-system the hope is not that things may go from bad to good but that they might go from good to better. Hope is not used as a compensation for suffering but as an indication of possibility and potential.

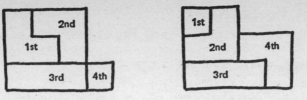

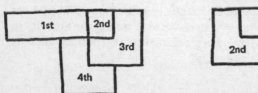

11

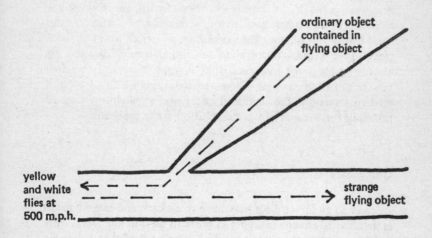

ordinary object
contained in
flying object

yellow
and white
flies at
500 m.p.h.

strange
flying object

12

Different ways of looking at things

Although a particular person may be moving along the main track someone else might have found the side track or even have been using the side track as his main track all along. This symbolizes the fact that different people may see the same thing in different ways, each of which is equally valid. This ties in with the tolerance of the new meta-system, based as it is on the humility of proto-truths which are never sufficiently regarded as absolute enough to be considered unique.

Moving away

The biodic symbol indicates an important and too-often-forgotten aspect of thinking and of evolution. If we have *gone* past the departure point of the side track, then further effort along the main track, no matter how intense it may be, will only take us even further away from the possibility of switching to the side track. This is quite opposite to our usual feeling that we are always on the right track and that further effort will therefore take us nearer to our goal. There are, today, very many aspects of modern society where increased effort and expenditure may be taking us further away from the solution of the problems.

Going back

In order to go forward we may have to go back and make a deliberate effort to change concepts in order to use the side track. This is why a change in concept may be more successful in solving a problem than a redoubling of effort. Too often we believe that our concepts must be right and all that is required is more effort in

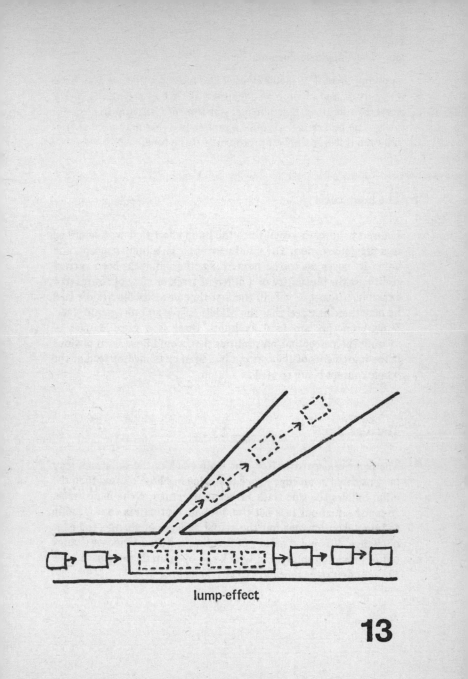

lump·effect

13

applying them. The biodic symbol also indicates that we may have to go back and change an idea even if that idea *was absolutely correct in its time*. It is not just a matter of changing inadequate ideas. The best of ideas is only a proto-truth that may need changing even if it was the best proto-truth at the time.

The lump effect

Figure 13 shows in visual form the lump effect that was described in a previous section. The mind may enter on a lump-concept, and when it moves on to the next thing, the mind has been carried right past the possibility of a different track or view of things. For example, if someone gets ill the first time he visits the Middle East he may thereafter feel that the Middle East is an unhygienic place. When concepts are used as lumps there is a great danger of missing the perceptual possibilities that would have been obvious if the ingredients of the concept had been examined instead of the whole concept being treated as a lump.

The edge effect

The point of departure from the main track to the side track may be considered as an edge. Once that edge has been crossed then the mind follows the side track rather than return to the main track. In many situations it is not the ultimate destination that is going to bring about change but the actual moment of change, the edge of change. It is not a matter of deciding the destination of change but of providing something which can open up the new path – *for the very first steps that have to be taken along it.*

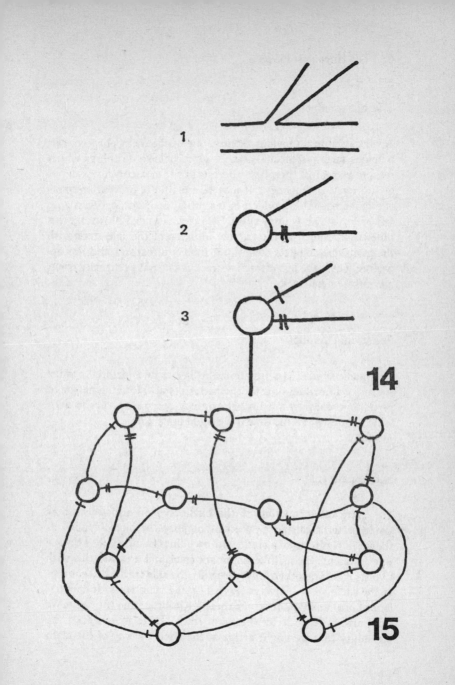

The hump effect

As discussed in a previous section, one of the main purposes of a religious meta-system has been to get people to do things which seem to go against their best interests at the moment (for example, giving away your money). It may be a matter of preventing someone doing something which is tempting, or making someone do something which is unpleasant. The biodic symbol illustrates this problem inasmuch as the narrow junction of the side track with the main one suggests something that is unnatural and less appealing, but if the less attractive track is taken it eventually opens out into a wider track.

Functional symbol

The biodic symbol is a functional rather than a pictorial symbol because it illustrates directly the pattern (track)-forming nature of perception and how a main pattern may obscure another pattern which is present all the time if we could but see it.

Stable patterns

The event-valve function of the biodic symbol also shows how stable patterns can arise. We can simplify the biodic symbol as shown in Figure 14 to a circle with two lines leading out of it. One line represents the main or dominant track and we mark this with two strokes. The other line represents the side track. If we arrive at the circle we will always leave it by the main track. It does not matter how many more tracks there are leading from the circle, we shall always leave it by the main track. There is, however, the possibility that we might arrive at the circle *by way of* the main track. By which of the other tracks do we then leave? We need to give a secondary degree of dominance to any one other track and this we do as shown in Figure 14 by marking it with one stroke. So in terms of leaving the circle the two-stroke track is dominant, but if this is unusable then the next preference is for the one-stroke track.

With this simple notation we can place a number of circles randomly on a piece of paper and connect them up by lines. The only restrictions are that each circle must have at least two lines going to it and that a line must always end in a circle. Within these limits you can make any number of connections you wish. The next stage is to go round each circle and mark one of the lines leaving it with two strokes and another with one stroke. When you have done this for all the circles the network is set. You now start with a pencil at any circle. You leave that circle by the two-stroke line and carry on to the next circle. You leave this in turn by the two-stroke line unless you have entered along that line in which case you leave by the one-stroke line. Just keep going. Whatever your initial arrangement you are bound to find that a track is established which repeats itself over and over again in a circular fashion (Figure 15).

If you try to start from a different circle you will be surprised to find how many starting-points lead into the same established track. Sometimes a new track is established. If, however, you change the dominance at one point (altering the strokes on the lines) a completely new track may become established.

This is only an exercise, but it does have a relevance to the way networks such as those in the brain can establish stable patterns.

Use of the biodic symbol

The symbol is something to be visualized and kept in mind as a constant reminder of the possibility of changing from the main track and discovering the side track that allows you to look at something in a new way.

Do not find your self by your shadow or your reflection but by the enjoyment with which you eat food and hear birds sing

When we consider that man is far and away the most wonderfully organized (or self-organized) system in the world we must be surprised at the little amount of respect he seems willing to give his self. Man is at the peak of nature's organizing power and yet he has tended to shun the self with which he has been provided as a matter of consciousness. Is it that man has felt himself to be so close to God that he was willing to advance himself even further by denying his earthy self? Or has it just been a yearning for a meta-system outside of himself because he fears that a system that indulged only in itself must be doomed? The fact is that the major religions of the world have sought strenuously to deny and attack man's self and to promise him salvation only if he rejected his own self. Quite apart from this there seems to be an urge on man's part to abdicate his own self to some higher authority, be it a group or the stars.

Christianity and self

The self was quickly recognized as the source of sin even before St Paul put the added emphasis on sex and sins of the flesh. The self was seen as selfish and greedy and prone to the seven deadly sins. The self was seen to be always out for immediate gratification with no thought for others or for the future. The self just wanted to have a good time and to resist everything except temptation. Amongst the deadly sins were self-love and pride.

The problem was that Christianity believed in personal salvation. There was to be free-will which would allow man to choose freely between good and evil. There had to be this free-will because he was going to be punished or rewarded depending on how he chose. There was to be a reckoning in the next life for which this one was but an antechamber. For the good there was heaven and the direct contemplation of God. For the wicked there was eternal hell-fire. Now of course there had to be a self which was going to exercise the free-will and be rewarded or punished according to the choices made.

The dilemma was solved in a most effective way. There would be the good self or the soul. Then there would be the bad self or the earthy self which was too interested in a good time on earth. The advantage of this device was that the bad self would provide a never-ending source of wickedness and evil which the good self could gain credit marks for overcoming. So a battle was set up within each person. Polarization soon followed, as it does in all conflict situations, and soon it came about that *anything* which the earthy self enjoyed was automatically evil and to be condemned. In fact there was merit to be gained by being especially nasty to the earthy self, using such means as starvation, flagellation and less extreme forms of self-denial. Each little victory over or subjugation of the bad self reinforced the will and strength of the good self. Not unnaturally, the bad self, like a caged prisoner who is never going to be rehabilitated, became badder and badder and took every opportunity of relaxed surveillance to indulge in a naughtiness that would not otherwise have been so appealing.

The lapses from perfection provided the fear and guilt which became so important a part of the Christian idiom. Since actual reward was rather remote, being located in heaven, there was a need for a more day-to-day control of behaviour. Fear and guilt provided this.

None of this practical operation of Christianity was implicit in the teachings of Christ himself. It just developed that way because of the mood of the times, the zeal and asceticism of the fathers of the Church and individuals like St Paul and St Augustine. St Augustine, for example, opposed the buoyant self-help principles of Pelagius because Pelagius was a heretic and so to be condemned, and also because self-help might make the Church somewhat superfluous. St Augustine was also pushed into the doctrine of original sin by a particular polemic.

And so it came about, perhaps with never a deliberate intention, that man had to choose between a self that could enjoy life and a God who had created life for man to enjoy but did not seem to want him to do so.

Buddhism and self

The Buddhists saw self differently. Self was the prime cause of man's earthly suffering. Self was greedy. Self was selfish towards other people. Self was hungry and thirsty and disappointed. Self felt pain. Instead of tackling each one of these problems separately, instead of offering a next-world compensation for the suffering as the Christians did (and so attempting to turn suffering into joy), the Buddhists decided that the most direct approach was to abolish self. This was not going to be easy because man was rather firmly embedded in his enjoyment of self. Unlike the Christians, the Buddhists did not want to subjugate the self. Instead of subjugation they chose detachment. Man was to detach himself from his self. The self was an illusion of pride and a creation of a mind that was always chopping up the continuum of the world into bite-sized morsels. Man's self was to sink back to become a part of nature. Man was to have no self but an awareness of the fact that he had no self.

In his archery training a Zen Buddhist monk is told not to aim at the target or to release the arrow. These things must happen by themselves as part of the flow of nature. The self must not get in the way with ambition, pride or disappointment. There is a story of a famous Zen monk who was about to be regarded as a 'grand master' until he failed on one point. It is said that he cried out as he was being murdered by a wayside thug. This showed insufficient detachment from what was going on. Buddhist novices are always told about the apparent dilemma of self. The more you go through the exercises and training the better *you* become at detachment from yourself. But there is not supposed to be a *you* to enjoy and take pride in your increasing skill in archery, sword-play, meditation or general detachment. But if there was not a *you* to make the effort and to aim for the ultimate goal of complete detachment, then the process would never have started in the first place. There must come a point at which the self is so detached from the self as not to be concerned about detachment at all. The dilemma is not a real one because it is the force of not-self which is so busy detaching itself from self. This is not unlike the good-self or soul of the Christian method.

There is a slight difference in the end-product. Christianity makes an effort to dispose of the greedy self. Buddhism makes an effort to dispose of the concerned self. But greediness is a form of concern just as concern is a form of greediness.

Marxism and self

Marxism solves the problem in an entirely different way. If selfishness is the problem of self, then selfishness should be abolished rather than self. This is achieved by creating a larger self called the State. Since the State is going to be supremely selfish there is no opportunity for anyone else to be selfish – and if they are it is a well-defined crime. Like the cells in a body each individual is to keep his prescribed place and role, bearing in mind that his function is to ensure the health and well-being of the State. Anything that puts the selfishness of an individual before the selfishness of the State is wrong. It is argued, quite plausibly, that the well-being of society must come before the well-being of its individual members. This is fairly obvious and even Christianity was concerned with the overall functioning of society as well as the salvation of individual souls. What is not so obvious in Marxism is that the well-being of the State (achieved through its selfishness) automatically ensures the well-being of the individuals other than those who are first in the queue for privileges. It can still be argued that one should not look at the present situation but at the future when the system will have had enough time to provide happiness for all its members.

The abdication of self

Where the self is not being consciously disposed of by means of a religious meta-system there is a tendency towards self-disposal of self by means of abdication. There is an abdication of the self to the mathematical dictates of the stars. There is an abdication of the self to the 'cause' or the 'doctrine' of the political group. There is an abdication of the self to drugs or alcohol which can provide more directly the pleasures the self would otherwise be seeking. There is an abdication of the self to a rigid set of social expectations and requirements that form a sort of carapace or outer-self for social viewing. There is an abdication of the self to psychoanalysis and the explained ingredients of self that have been supplied by early traumas. There is an abdication of the self to genes and social deprivation. The abdication ranges from: 'Not me but God through me' to 'Not me but my genetic coding.'

The deep self

Ever since Freud suggested that what happened in the conscious mind was only a socially acceptable version of the more evil, and interesting, things that happened in the subconscious mind there has been a tendency for psychologists and others to suppose that the truth lies deep. The deeper you could dig the more truth you were going to uncover. That you do discover something that was not visible on the surface does not, of course, make it the truth. A mining engineer who sinks his shaft right through a surface seam of coal has only his prejudice to console him that the deeper he digs the more coal he will find. Beauty is often only skin deep and if we strip away the surface layers of skin we will not find something more beautiful underneath. We will find muscles and bone which are different and just as important in their own way. It may just be that people are better on the surface, that the surface personality made up of consciousness, habits and inhibitions moulded by individual experience into an individual is more important than the uniformity of the deep self which is more or less the same in everyone. The deep-self vogue so fashionable in America is really only another example of abdication, the abdication of the conscious self to unconscious forces as described in psychology manuals.

Burden or joy

Is self a burden or a joy? The above paragraphs suggest that many people in history and today regard self as a burden, as a source of evil or at least as a bore. The new meta-system is committed to regarding self not only as a joy but as the main point of man's existence. There is a point at which self-love is dignity and not arrogance. There is a point at which selfishness is the culture of self and not greed at the expense of others. There is a point at which the ego no longer needs self-inflation. The new meta-system is aimed at each of these points. If the goal is hard to reach at least it seems more worth-while than the denial or abdication of self. It is possible that if we let free at last the caged prisoner of self he will come to enjoy his freedom and peace more than his appetites. We must be aware of the lump effect of words like selfish, self-important, self-centred. If we exercise the right balance in the right framework they represent worth-while objectives. After all, what is more selfish than a Christian working to get his soul to heaven or a Buddhist seeking release from the cycle of life?

A man should fill his skin

A child's play-pen defines the space in which he can play around. A factory occupies a space and so does an airfield or a town or a nature reserve. An electric fire radiates effective warmth over a limited space. A telephone exchange serves a limited space even though it may be connected up to other exchanges elsewhere. Space is an area in which something happens. A space does not have to be defined by boundaries: it may be the intensity of the happening within the space that defines the space. We can draw an imaginary boundary around some type of activity and call the area within the boundary the activity-space. This means that for practical purposes the activity can be regarded as happening in that space. The activity is not bounded or restricted by the space, as is a child in a play-pen. If the activity moves elsewhere then the boundary moves with it and the activity-space is still the same activity-space but located elsewhere. The hunting range of a lion or tiger is defined by a radius of some miles around wherever he may be: that is his activity-space.

Life-space

A child's physical life-space is carefully defined by his parents and his school. His mental life-space may be much less restricted but still deals with matters based on his own experience. A philosopher's life-space may be much wider – ranging in terms of interests and experiences but not much larger physically. Life-space refers to the *operating-space* in which a person operates or is expected to operate. Just as each individual person is a unique system so the interaction of that individual system with the general system of the world around defines the operating-space. This operating-space may be set by circumstances. A schoolmaster, a factory employee and an airline stewardess all have definite operating-spaces defined by their work. But the operating-space includes the total system interaction and not just the physical limits. So the attitude to other people at work, the attitude to work itself and the emotions involved all become part of the operating-space or life-space. The circumstances that are included in the operating-space may be real (having to prepare the accounts) or imagined (imagining that the boss does not like you). The operating-space is the perceptual-space: that is to say, the way we look at the part of the world in which we have to operate. This, like any other perception, is based on reality but may present an individual picture of it. The life-space or operating-space is the space in which as individuals we are expected – or expect ourselves – to operate. It is the total set of expectations that define the operating-space. Because of these expectations (self-imposed or imposed by circumstances) the life-space or operating-space may be called the demand-space. *The demand-space includes all the demands that life seems to make upon each individual.*

The expressions 'life-space', 'operating-space' and 'demand-space' can be used interchangeably. Each gives a slightly different aspect of the same situation. Life-space implies that part of life in which an individual actually lives. Operating-space implies the space in which an individual operates. Demand-space implies the demands made by the total set of expectations that define the operating-space.

Self-space

Self-space is quite different from life-space and usually much smaller. Self-space can be called the 'cope-space'. *Self-space is that part of the life-space with which a person can cope easily and without effort.* That is to say, the part of the life-space that has become part of the person's own system so that it is no longer a demand made upon that system.

Self-space is within a person's control. It is the part of the life-space with which an individual can cope with enjoyment, confidence and happiness. It is as much part of him as his nose or blowing his nose. Just as a person's real skin defines the outer boundary of his physical self so an imaginary skin includes under it the self-space of an individual.

A man should fill his own skin. In his self-space a person should not be dependent on any other person for his happiness. There may be physical dependence, as in the case of a cripple who has to be helped, but there should be no emotional dependence in the self-space. This is not to imply an aloofness or detachment or a rejection of loving relationships. On the contrary, such relationships can only work if they arise between two 'selves' or 'self-spaces' which are themselves independent.

For the same reasons the self-space should not depend on 'shadow' or 'reflection'. That is to say, the awareness of self should not depend on the power or influence exerted over other people – nor should it depend on the approval or praise of other people. A self which only exists in the approval of the world or other individuals is not a real self. A self which only exists in terms of the alterations it causes in the world is no real self. The thrashings of a swimmer are not the swimmer. The sting of a wasp is not the wasp. The exhaust roar of a motorcycle is not the motorcycle. A self should be more than a collection of photos of the self in action.

Self-space is *dignity* space. It is the space within which a person is at ease with himself and with his circumstances. Within his self-space a person is at ease. There is no striving to create a self or to express it. The self is actuality in the self-space. Just as the taste of a chocolate ice-cream is the taste of a chocolate ice-cream so the self is content to be the self in its self-space. The self-space defines the self which can respect itself and for which others can respect it. There is no shame, pretence or window-dressing.

The self-space is not defined by perfection or excellence. The self-space boundary is not drawn to include only those admirable aspects of a person's nature. The self-space includes warts and all. The self-space is human. The one defining characteristic of the self-space is *ease*. It is that part of the demand-space with which a person can cope with ease.

The gap

Figures 16 and 17 show some life-space maps in which the area covered by the self-space varies. In one case there may be a large demand-space and a relatively small self-space. In another case the demand-space is smaller and the self-space fills it more fully. In yet another case a large self-space occupies much of a large demand-space.

In looking at the relationship between life space and self-space we can concentrate on the gap between the two, or the unfilled part of the life-space. For this purpose it is easier to talk in terms of demand-space and cope-space. The ratio between cope-space and demand-space will indicate how well the self-space fills the life-space. We can then talk of the cope/demand ratio. Usually this will be less than one, because, as our self-space expands, our ambitions and expectations tend to enlarge the life-space as well.

It must be obvious that when the cope/demand ratio is low the gap between the life-space and self-space must be large. When the cope/demand ratio approaches unity the gap narrows. What does this gap mean?

Pressure and opportunity

The gap between cope-space and demand-space (self-space and life-space) defines pressure or opportunity. It defines either the pressures that are exerted on an individual or the opportunity or challenge that is open to an individual. Since opportunity is positive and pressure is negative it is important to be able to distinguish between the two

Deciding whether the gap is a pressure gap or an opportunity gap is a matter for individual thinking and perception and is one of the tasks expected of an individual in the new meta-system. Some guidelines can, however, be given:

Whether the gap is positive or negative may depend on the temperament of an individual. Some enjoy challenge, some enjoy peace.

The gap may change its appearance from positive to negative from day to day depending on the mood of the moment.

If the gap has been there for a *long time* and there has been no success in reducing it then it seems more sensible to regard it as a pressure than as an opportunity.

If a person considers himself to be unhappy then the gap is quite definitely a pressure. Happiness is defined as an approach towards a cope/demand ratio of unity: an exact fit between cope and demand.

Self-improvement

The room for a conscious effort towards happiness is to be found in the pressure-opportunity gap, and the process will be described in a later section. Life-spaces and self-spaces are rarely static. They are usually expanding or contracting, depending on external circumstances and internal moods. Suggestions for altering both life-space and self-space are given later in this book.

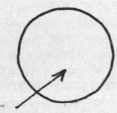

life-space
(demand-space)

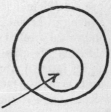

self-space
(cope-space)

16

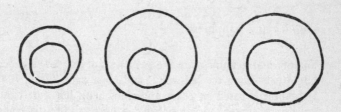

different proportions of self & life-spaces

17

Different life-spaces

So far this section has dealt with an overall or average life-space map which an individual ought to be able to draw for himself. It is also possible to draw one for someone else or have a friend draw one for you. Ultimately, however, it is your own view of things that matters most.

It is possible to draw life-space maps for the *different selves* that have to cope with different aspects of life. These different selves are the different roles which an individual is called upon to fill. There can be an 'external' life-space map which deals with the individual's reaction to the external world. Then there is an 'internal' life-space map which deals with an individual's reaction to his internal world. There can also be life-space maps dealing with marriage, family, work, the community and the world at large. Figure 18 shows a whole family of such life-space maps. In the case of this individual it is easy to see that he is happiest when working on his hobby.

For each life-space map it is important to realize that life-space is defined by the total demands or expectations made by the world and by oneself. The self-space is defined by that part of the demand-space that can be coped with in ease and peace.

Dignity and happiness

Dignity and happiness are the twin aims of the new meta-system. Dignity is based on self-worth and on a man 'filling his skin'. Happiness is based on peace and enjoyment. Both are closely related to an understanding of what happens to life-space and self-space.

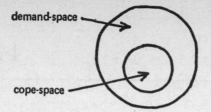

WORK

HOBBY

FAMILY

FRIENDS

COMMUNITY

18

Just as burning is the proper function of fire so happiness is the proper function of man's existence

It has been stated quite clearly at the beginning of this book that in the new meta-system happiness is regarded as the legitimate purpose of man's existence. Happiness is regarded as the proper functioning of the system we call man.

It was stated in the preceding section that the twin aims of the new meta-system were happiness and dignity. In fact dignity is only a special form of happiness: it is happiness with one's self.

In the new meta-system it is happiness here and now that matters. It is not happiness promised in some after-life or after-detachment from the cares of the world. It must be realized, however, that happiness here and now does *not* of itself exclude happiness in whatever after-life a particular belief system proposes. It may well be argued that Christianity was really concerned with happiness in this life because it made suffering bearable. It may be argued that until distorted by individual attitudes Christianity was about happiness in this life as well. There are those who feel that Pope John XXIII had a truer understanding of this than had many churchmen in history.

The aim, goal, objective and destination of the new meta-system is individual happiness.

Deliberate happiness

To some people it may seem a contradiction in terms that there should be an *effort* towards happiness. To try to culture happiness may seem to destroy that elusive mood. There are those who will always feel that anguish and ecstasy and suffering and bliss must be allowed to take their spontaneous place in the nature of human existence – as unprogrammed as thunder and lightning and as fleeting as a rainbow. There are those who will feel that any attempt to capture happiness must have the same effect as forgoing the beauty of wild flowers by the wayside in favour of formal gardens. This is a romantic idiom which has much merit and should never be discarded. Romance is made for dreams and dreams are an essential ingredient of happiness. But the *laissez-faire* attitude to happiness is too wasteful, too negligent and too selfish. Very few people ever have the chance to enjoy except for brief moments the spontaneous happiness of the roadside wild flowers. And in any case that is not being abandoned. Today, flowers by the wayside will only be preserved if we make a deliberate effort to preserve them. The world has become complex and the pressures are great and confusing. They do not disappear because a few people can remove themselves to still lyrical parts of the countryside. Most people have to cope with a world which they might wish to be simpler and more lyrical, but without an effort on their part the world will *not* spontaneously move in this direction.

Townspeople often show a disregard for nature or at least a lack of appreciation. Country people feel that sensitivity to nature needs to be developed by attention and exposure. In the same way a sensitivity to happiness needs to be developed by attention and exposure.

Too often in our usual 'lump-effect' approach we tend to think of anything deliberate as being mechanical and ugly. But art is deliberate, even if the final effect is lyrical and spontaneous. We can contrast the English country garden, with its wildly romantic settings that are even more romantic than nature could manage, with the formal geometry of French classical gardens to realize that deliberate attention can enhance beauty and not destroy it.

Many people know that certain dishes will give them indigestion. They know that other dishes will give them pleasure. Should they then sit down at a table in a restaurant and use a chance method to select the menu because a deliberate choice will ruin their enjoyment? There are certain circumstances that make people happy and others that make people unhappy (like complex forms, regimentation and tax demands). Should we abandon any distinction between these different sorts of circumstance and make no effort to ensure that we have more of the pleasurable ones and less of the unpleasant ones? The people who advocate spontaneous happiness usually take care to place themselves in circumstances that are more likely to provide it.

There is no reason why we should be passive about happiness. We can make a conscious effort to value it and develop sensitivity to it and encourage those circumstances which provide it.

Types of happiness

Happiness is quite properly a vague and general word that needs no tight definition since such a definition would add nothing to the understanding of its meaning. If a person feels that he is happy, then he is happy. We can, however, look at some of the alternative types of happiness or the ingredients that from time to time are believed to contribute to happiness.

Pleasure Pleasure is very real. There is the pleasure of friends, of beauty, of food, of drink, of humour, of achievement and of physical exercise. Pleasure is so real that we can insert an electrode into a rat's brain and stimulate the 'pleasure centre' directly and deliberately. One day we may be able to do this for man. In a way, with drugs we can almost do it now. It is this rather mechanical nature of pleasure which has gotten it a bad reputation. Those religions that have sought to deny the self have done it on the basis that the self is naturally pleasure-seeking and as a consequence greedy, selfish and self-indulgent. It is this excess of pleasure-seeking which has been seen as sinful and which has led to condemnation of any pleasure-seeking. The natural purpose of pleasure has been seen as the sugar coating on the pill to make man do the things that were necessary for his survival as an organic system: food, drink, sex, etc. Over-indulgence in pleasure is rather like a child opening the bathroom cabinet and eating all the sweet-tasting red iron pills because of the sugar coating – and then suffering the very dangerous iron poisoning. If there was a natural cut-off to pleasure – as there is to some extent in eating and drinking – there would be nothing to condemn. In the absence of a natural cut-off, man has to develop some *sense of balance*. It is towards the development of such a sense of balance that the new meta-system is inclined rather than a condemnation of pleasure as such.

Excitement   Excitement, like pleasure, is another danger area. Novelty soon wears off and the seeking of excitement demands more and more effort. The search for stimulation and novelty gets more difficult. The periods between the excitements grow ever more boring. Boredom is *created* by excitement, not by the lack of it. It is the hankering for excitement, the memory of it and the troughs between peaks of excitement that create boredom. A country-dweller who becomes acquainted with the excitements of the town can now develop a boredom towards the country. Excitement creates boredom as surely as pleasure creates indigestion. What is the alternative? Should we eschew excitement in favour of a life of tranquil peace and contentment relying on developed sensitivities to provide pleasure? It is fair to argue that pleasure and excitement are actually counter-productive because they blunt the senses and so make it more and more difficult to achieve the same effect. It is quite impossible to recapture the thrill of driving a motor car on one's own for the first time, or having one's first book published. The first kiss of a romance is always the best. Is it possible to sensitize the mind so that the arrival of any stranger at a remote country farm becomes as exciting as the party-of-the-century for a socialite? If we really treasure excitement then perhaps we need to cultivate it very, very carefully.

Enthusiasm The Greek word comes from a 'joining with God' or being carried along by a spirit of involvement. Enthusiasm is the opposite of apathy and as such must be life-enhancing. Enthusiasm can be attached to anything by a person who is willing to be enthusiastic. Unlike pleasure and excitement, enthusiasm is not counter-productive without balance. Possibly there is a danger of too rapid a switching of interests to whatever new excites the new enthusiasm. There is also the danger of waiting to be carried along on a wave of enthusiasm and being unable to invest effort and interest in something if the enthusiasm is not there.

Joy Joy is pleasure of a more aesthetic and intellectual type. Whereas the circumstances that arouse pleasure are recognized and dependable – until satiety sets in – the circumstances that arouse joy may be recognized but not easily produced on demand. It may be a change of circumstances that produces joy or a special combination of circumstance and mood. There would not seem to be any danger in an over-indulgence in joy – indeed Christian saints were said to be in a permanent state of joyful contemplation of God.

Interest An expert builds up an interest in a subject. An expert in antique furniture will get pleasure out of looking at antique furniture or in extending his knowledge. A collector develops interest in what he is collecting and the interest is a permanent source of pleasure. Interest seems to be a means to the end of joy or pleasure, but that is only because of our language inadequacy which must describe anything enjoyable as 'joy' or 'pleasure'. Interest is a distinct source of happiness in itself. It is also the most durable, dependable and permanent.

Relief Freedom from fear and worry; freedom from guilt; freedom from pressures all make for relief. It is true that the happiness of relief tends to be brief and only covers the sudden relief from the previous discomfort (or when the discomfort is re-created in memory). When people sneer at cow-like contentment they are sneering at a form of happiness that seems to be based on the *negative* wish to be relieved of the pressure of involvement in life. Relief from a headache is pleasurable until the headache is forgotten. In the modern world relief from complexity and confusion is a real happiness. Relief from having to make a difficult decision is also a real happiness. So relief involves the removal of those pressures that give rise to unhappiness.

Peace The contentment of peace is more than just absence of discomfort. It is more than just relief. It is more than complacency and smugness. In functional terms peace is the proper functioning of the human system and is as recognizable as the proper functioning of a motor-car engine: everything is in its place and fulfilling its role; there is no excess friction or strain. Left to itself, nature is at peace with itself.

Now-care and future-care

The religious meta-systems have felt that if man were left to himself he would seek only the gratification of the moment: he would concentrate on the pleasure of now-care instead of investing in future-care. It was felt that he would tend to exploit his present situation to the fullest for its pleasure content rather than try and improve the situation: he would spend his Friday night wages on getting drunk instead of saving to buy a better house. It was supposed that man would be irresponsible in his search for pleasure, preferring instant pleasure to future pleasure. These suppositions are probably correct for many people. But they can be corrected by a longer-term view of happiness as an objective instead of dismissing it as an objective. The balance between now-care and future-care is an area of difficulty: it requires awareness and conscious effort. To tackle the problem by denying happiness as a legitimate objective is like a doctor treating an infected arm by amputation – on the basis that if the arm is no longer there it cannot give any trouble. The aim of the new meta-system is a proper pursuit of happiness. Proper simply means *effective*. If it is effective to have a balance between now-care and future-care, then that is to be preferred to concentration only on one or the other.

Balance

It must have become obvious by now that the problem of happiness is the problem of balance. This a problem both of our perception and of our language because we prefer to deal with polarized situations and either/or decisions. Yet in the world of business and management the problem of balance has to be tackled in a definite manner. To make this easier the concepts of 'cut-off' and 'trade-off' have been developed. Cut-off implies that something may be worth-while up to a point but not beyond that point. So a hotel management may spend money on making a hotel more luxurious, but there is a cut-off point beyond which it is not worth spending more money. So pleasure may contribute to happiness up to a point, but beyond that point it may be counter-productive and make happiness more difficult. Trade-off implies that one thing may have to be given up or 'traded' for another. A toy manufacturer would like to make his toy more interesting but the cost of manufacture would rise, so he has to exercise a trade-off between interest and cost. Similarly an individual may have consciously to exercise a trade-off between the need for excitement and peace. There is no reason why he should not base this on his experience or on how successful he is at either.

The problem of balance is also the problem of adjustment and change. How far does a person adjust himself to his situation and how far does he try to change his situation? The answer to this problem has a major influence on happiness.

The basic problem of balance is dealt with in detail in a later section.

Action

What sort of action can an individual take in order to increase his happiness? This aspect will also be dealt with in a later section.

There must be an element of awareness of one's own temperament and of past experiences. Skill in happiness is based like any other skill on experience and self-observation. There is a place for the development of will-power and discipline and also for sensitization through deliberate training.

It is probably not possible ever to induce happiness by an effort of will. But an individual can generate or choose circumstances which themselves can generate happiness. An individual can also work on his perceptions so that he comes to look at things in a different way. So circumstances can be changed, or the perception of circumstances.

A person dieting can choose either to take a little food or to take a lot and then deliberately leave some on his plate. In the pursuit of happiness there is considerable scope for action and choice. It is not a matter of passively hoping that happiness will happen like a rainbow in the sky.

Adjustments of the cope/demand ratio between self-space and life-space is a further area of activity that will be discussed in another section.

Ups and downs

We know that mood is quite closely controlled by chemicals in the hypothalamus part of the brain. These can increase or decrease in amount depending on stress and other things. Mood will follow the variations in these chemicals. Most people experience ups and downs. In addition to identifying situations which may exaggerate these swings, and in addition to trying to smooth them out, an individual may need to acknowledge them. He need not feel that if his mood is depressed on a particular day his pursuit of happiness has failed. He should acknowledge that the mood will pass. He may need to adjust his life according to his moods. The moods are certainly not regular enough to be predicted by a mechanical device that calculates forwards from the date of birth. Natural rhythms could not possibly be that predictable, for a few days out here or there would soon upset any prediction. The rhythms of a woman's menstrual cycle are a classic example of a physiological rhythm and these could not be predicted years in advance from the date of birth (or even puberty). So the artificial character of currently fashionable 'Bio-rhythms' can serve like astrology as a framework to be believed in rather than a reflection of the body's activities. Nevertheless, a consciousness of the chemically-based fluctuations in mood is important in the pursuit of happiness.

Limitations

It may seem that the conscious pursuit of happiness must lead to a selfish hedonism with all its dangers. The restrictions that are necessary to protect against these dangers will be discussed in a later section. It is enough to say here that they are of two types: (a) the consideration of others and avoiding interference with their own right to pursue happiness; and (b) the effectiveness of the pursuit and acknowledgement that some activities can be counter-productive unless controlled by balance.

If nothing is really worth doing then everything is worth doing well because activity provides its own worth

Man is a living organism. Being alive involves two things. The first is being able to respond – being responsive – living. The second is being able to act – being active – being lively. Both being responsive and acting are really types of activity. We can distinguish two types of activity. In a tennis match there is the activity of the server who is serving but there is also the activity of the person who is waiting to receive service. The receiver is on his toes and fully active but not actually doing anything. We can further compare the two types of activity to the activity of an animal and the activity of a plant. The animal prowls and hunts and preys. The plant is immobile but active according to its own nature.

Apathy and activity

It is easiest to define activity by defining its opposite. The opposite of activity is passivity: not doing anything but waiting for it to happen. The opposite of activity is apathy: a lack of interest in anything because nothing can be seen as important enough to do. The opposite of activity is time-filling: sitting in front of a television set because this makes it unnecessary to think of anything else to do.

Boredom

For many people today boredom is a much bigger problem than suffering. Meta-systems that were designed to deal with suffering are not especially effective at dealing with boredom. There is boredom because life is easy. There is boredom because achievement is difficult without effort and effort is too much trouble. There is boredom because passive entertainment and time-filling devices have reached a high level of development. There is boredom because there is less danger and less involvement in society. There is boredom because there is a higher demand for synthetic excitement and second-hand excitement through mass entertainment.

Action activity

This is the usual meaning of the term 'activity'. It means doing something, bringing something about. It may be embroidery or angling or golf or politics or bricklaying or mountain climbing. The new meta-system is in favour of activity *even for the sake of activity* – provided the activity is not an excuse to avoid doing other things, thus becoming a time-filling exercise. If activity is an end in itself then it follows that whatever is done is worth doing well whether it be scrambling an egg or playing the violin. If nothing really seems worth doing then everything is worth doing well. It is the interaction of the activity and the self that matters. Activity is self in action. It is the enjoyment of this self-in-action that is the purpose of the activity.

Awareness activity

An old lady in a Greek village sits quietly by the side of the road for hours. She is still, but her eyes are darting about noticing everything and absorbing it – perhaps appreciating life around her. Awareness is a form of activity. Observation and appreciation are forms of activity. Activity need not always involve beavering around but can involve the mental activity of awareness. If you are walking through a wood the activity of your walking is only a small part of your total activity of enjoyment and observation. Is watching a football match activity? It can be when it is not just time-filling. But football is a game to be played rather than watched. Deliberate television viewing can be activity but time-filling television watching is not. Awareness activity really involves more effort than action activity because awareness activity needs to be deliberately chosen for its own sake and not through laziness. To really read a book is a high degree of activity – to read the words and turn the pages is no activity at all.

Achievement

All activity involves achievement. But there can be two sorts of achievement. There is the achievement of destination and there is the achievement of performance. In the achievement of destination it is *getting* to a certain place that matters: like trying to set the world non-stop record for table tennis. In the achievement of performance it is the actual performance that matters: a skier does not ski because he wants to get to the bottom of the hill but because he wants to enjoy the performance. When Churchill painted his pictures or laid bricks in the famous wall in his garden it was the achievement of performance that mattered. In many situations the two things go together. An author writing a book wants to get to the end but he might also enjoy writing the book.

A builder may wish to finish the building but he may also enjoy the actual building. Throughout the ages many have been the exhortations that it is the journey that matters more than the destination but in spite of this we still tend to think of achievement in terms of destination. This may be because in a competitive world it is the destination (the extra university degree or admired masterpiece) that wins the competition; it is the destination that establishes ourselves in the eyes of our fellows; it is the destination that is rewarded in cash. In the new meta-system yet another attempt is made to put the emphasis on the achievement of *performance* rather than the achievement of destination. The two are not incompatible, but if an unenjoyable effort is sustained purely to achieve a particular destination then the activity is worthless. If the effort itself is enjoyed then it does not make it less enjoyable if it has a definite destination. One should be able to enjoy cycling instead of just using a cycle as a means of getting somewhere. One should be able to enjoy the company of another without wondering what one is going to get out of it. Destinations are never very satisfactory because, like excitement, they only set a further task.

Achievement and life-space

Figure 19 shows the different self-spaces and life-spaces of an individual. It is clear that in the work situation the cope/demand ratio is very low. In the family situation it is also rather low. But in the hobby area (rose growing?) the cope/demand ratio approaches the happiness ratio of unity. Activity with which you can cope easily *becomes part* of the self-space. It does not matter that you have chosen the activity simply because you can cope with it. Activity of this sort can have three beneficial effects:

Oasis of competence There is at least one 'self' which is happy. The activity area can become a sort of oasis for the self in its retreat from those areas with which it cannot cope so well.

Confidence The cope/demand ratio in this special area of activity can be carried over to other areas. It has been noticed in

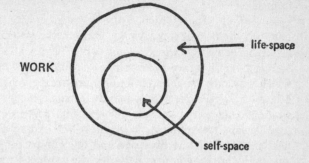

WORK

life-space

self-space

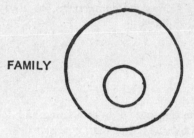

FAMILY

HOBBY

19

school that if children who are lacking in confidence are given an opportunity to excel in one area then the confidence that is built up extends to other areas with a marked improvement in performance.

Ratio-effect The addition of the new area of activity actually improves the overall cope/demand ratio in the general life-space map. This happens in the following way. The new area of activity increases the life-space because there are now new expectations which may take the form either of opportunities or of pressures. But the activity is one with which the person can cope easily so it serves to enlarge the self-space. For example, we can consider a cope/demand ratio of one half which we will express as 5: 10. We now enlarge both the life-space and the self-space by the same amount by bringing in new activities: the result is $5 + 2: 10 + 2$, or $7 :12$. It can be seen that the ratio has improved.

Enjoying doing things and doing them has always been a dependable road to happiness.

Direction

Achievement is setting out to do something and doing it. There has to be a definite focus rather than a passive drift. The doer has to decide what he wants to achieve or enjoy. It is no different from directing attention from one part of a painting to another. Anything can become an area for achievement, an area for enjoyment of activity.

Helping other people has long been a traditional achievement area in the Christian meta-system. It remains a powerful opportunity area for achievement.

Hobbies and special interests are already the main achievement area for many people. Learning and specialization in a field also come into this group. So do connoisseurship and collecting. The danger is that of the destination becoming the only important thing.

Work is the most obvious achievement area since it takes up so much time anyway, and yet in many cases it has simply become a time-filling activity. This is partly the result of the boredom and lack of involvement of much work but also the result of the notion that work is one of the sufferings of life and not a source of enjoyment.

Organization and community work is another obvious area of activity. The second part of this book offers some specific opportunities for this.

Inner-world activity

So far in this section the emphasis has been placed on activity in the outer world. There should, however, be a balance so that there is also some activity in the inner world. It would be quite wrong to put all the emphasis on inner-world activity and reject outer-world activity, for two reasons: because the world would not be benefited in any way; because outer-world activity is more dependable as a source of happiness than inner-world activity. In practice there is not as sharp a separation between outer-world activity and inner-world activity as is suggested here. Quite often outer-world activity is deliberately undertaken because in itself it provides inner-world activity: for example, playing a musical instrument. The balance between outer-world activity and inner-world activity must depend on individual preference tempered by effort and even discipline.

Inner-world activity involves thinking: both to solve problems and to *enjoy the sheer activity of thinking*. Inner-world activity involves a state of self-awareness. This self-awareness is a quiet observation of oneself and the internal world. It is a sort of audit or examination of the state of affairs. It is not a matter of concentrating on faults or an examination of conscience. It is being able to draw a life-space map and not be worried about it.

Inner-world activity can also involve the important activity of re-examining perceptions and making attempts to change them. The problem of adjustment to circumstances or the change of circumstances as a means to happiness has been mentioned at several points already. Adjustment to circumstances may involve a change in the outer world but it is more likely to involve a change in the perception of some part of that world. A change in circumstances will almost certainly involve activity in the external world, but it can be preceded by new ideas generated in the internal world.

Reactive activity and projective activity

Reactive activity is activity brought about as a reaction to something that has happened in the life-space. An individual is called upon to react to it. It may be an order he has to obey or a problem that he has to solve. It is possible to adopt an attitude of mind that makes even reactive activity a source of enjoyable achievement: do it smartly, do it well, do it simply, do it effectively. But activity should not be confined to reactive activity even when there is a lot of this. There is more enjoyment and achievement to be had in projective activity: in setting out to do something on your own initiative because you want to.

High-achievers and competition

The emphasis in this section on activity and achievement may have given the false impression that the new meta-system was designed to create a lot of highly competitive, high-achieving neurotics. Exactly the opposite is the case. High-achieving expectations and competitive expectations only serve to enlarge the life-space *without* enlarging the self-space (until complete success follows). The result is to make for a decrease in the cope/demand ratio and an increase in unhappiness. Competition is only useful as a device to overcome passivity and apathy. Competition, as in sport, is enjoyable and of use to those who enjoy it. Self-space should never depend on competitive success.

The goals set for achievement are more practical as attainable, 'bite-sized' goals than as unattainable star-high ideals. This is not to exclude aiming high but to suggest that it should be restricted to those whose temperament can cope with it. A long journey that is broken up into smaller sections is much more enjoyable on the way – and it is this enjoyment on the way that matters.

World involvement

Unlike several other meta-systems, the new meta-system encourages *active involvement* in world affairs whether in business or politics. These areas can become activity and enjoyment areas. The only caution is that they should not be used as ego supports because this will become counter-effective. A person who needs to achieve something in order to be happy has a counter-effective strategy: he is simply enlarging his life-space and leaving his self-space to occupy an even smaller part of it (so decreasing the cope/demand ratio).

Dignity is not measured by the value of the self-space but by its coincidence with the ego

A man has dignity when he is happy with himself – not because others have suggested that he should be but because he is. A man has dignity *when his image of his own self-space coincides with his real self-space*. That is to say when his self-space and his *ego* are the same. This is suggested in Figure 20. A man has happiness when his self-space coincides with his life-space.

Since self-space has already been defined as that part of his life-space with which a person can cope with ease, dignity means an ego that is at ease. An ego that is always pushing for recognition and inflating itself is not at ease. It has no dignity. Such an ego is larger than the self-space and has led to an enlargement of the life-space (through its own expectations and consequent pressures), leaving the true self-space as small as ever.

If a man wants to acquire dignity he has only to shrink, or enlarge, his ego to match his self-space.

Arrogance and selfishness are really sins not of self but of communication. Arrogance implies a lack of responsiveness to others, and selfishness implies activity at the expense of others. With regard to the self there can only be confidence or pretension. Confidence is the dignity referred to above: a man has the right to be confident over matters with which he can easily cope. Pretension is the over-inflation of the ego referred to above.

The value of self-space

The actual value of the self-space matters not at all
The self-space of a baker is as valuable as the self-sp.   .e
President of France. It is the actuality of the self-space tha. .iatters
and the quiet confidence that arises from this actuality that gives
rise to dignity: the ratio 100 : 100 is the same as 7 : 7.

It may be remarked that a criminal whose ego coincided with
his self-space would then have dignity. The answer is that he
would. In itself criminality does not contravene any rules of self.
What it does contravene is the relationship between individuals
and between an individual and society. This aspect is discussed
more fully in a later section. It is enough to say here that one of
the few 'sins' condemned by the new meta-system is that of
system-cheat – or someone who takes advantage of a system: a
system-parasite.

A drunk, quite apart from making demands on others, would go
against the principle of self because drunkenness is a form of self-
abdication. The coping space or self-space of a drunk would necessarily be rather small. Yet a drunk could have his dignity.

Plurality

In the new meta-system the aim is not towards perfection. The
aim is not towards the perfect, well-balanced, well-rounded Re-
naissance man. There is a recognition that there are all sorts and
shapes and sizes of temperament and personality. It is pointless,
and dull, to suppose that with enough improvement each of us
would reach a bland state of uniform perfection. It is the individuality of an individual which makes him a unique system on
his own.

Dignity means being happy in one's own self-space. That automatically involves a recognition of the nature of one's indi-

...duality – or peculiarity. True style is the combination of individuality and dignity. The eccentric has dignity because he is at ease with his eccentricity. The flamboyant attention-grabber is not at ease because he *needs* the attention he may or may not get. Even if he is skilled enough to be sure of getting it each time, he still needs it – and the self-space must be *independent* of needs outside of oneself.

Different people are good at different things. The new meta-system puts an emphasis on this plurality of personality and talent because it puts an emphasis on self. Any creed that denies self tends to deny individual varieties of self. The organization outlined in the last part of this book acknowledges a plurality of types.

Self-improvement

Using the definitions of the new meta-system, self-improvement would seem to involve either an enlargement of the self-space or a shrinking of the life-space or a combination of both. This matter is dealt with in more detail in a later section, but some indications are given here.

With most people the life-space is too large. People are *bullied by opportunities* as much as by pressures. There are expectations and ambitions and the complex demands of modern life. To some extent the life-space can be shrunk and this is a direction for effort. The alternative is to enlarge the self-space. There are various ways in which this can be done.

Increasing control The part of the life-space over which a person is in control and therefore at ease can be enlarged by training and by deliberate application.

Detachment A person can be at ease with part of the life-space over which he has no control by a process of detachment and not-minding. Since he is now at ease in this area, his self-space enlarges.

Actual change By bringing about an actual change in circum-

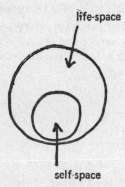

life-space

self-space

near happiness

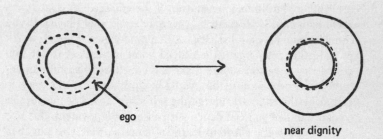

ego

near dignity

20

stances which allows the person to be at ease with a new section of the life-space. (In practice, this is more often a matter of changing the life-space rather than enlarging the self-space.)

Perceptual change   A deliberate and successful effort to change a perception can lead to a considerable enlargement of the self-space. For example, the conquest of phobias and over-reactive patterns can greatly increase self-space.

Discipline   By conscious effort a person may be able to sustain a changed attitude even though there has been no perceptual change. The degree of effort required may seem to go against the concept of 'ease' on which the self-space is based, but the ease refers to ease of coping or effectiveness of coping.

Oscillations

The enlarged self-space may only be held for a short time, after which it collapses again. This does not matter. Improvement does not have to be continuous. There may be a continuous oscillation in a sort of Jekyll and Hyde manner. With time it becomes easier to sustain the enlarged self-space. It will, of course, seem that the enlarged self-space is just an act that can be put on for short periods and that the true self remains in its old confines. This is probably so, but it does not matter. If the enlarged self-space gives more happiness it is worth it – even as a role well played. If you can with ease play a role that gives happiness then it is well worth playing that role. Again the crucial point is 'ease'. It is not suggested that a person should make a great effort to sustain an enlarged self-space because that would be contradictory. But a person can make the effort to *enlarge* the self-space. It is not pleasurable to dance unless you can dance with ease and enjoyment. But it is worth making the effort to learn to dance so that you can then dance with ease and enjoyment. It is not worth sitting in discomfort on a badly designed chair but it is worth making some effort to find a chair that suits you so that you can then sit in comfort. Thus an enlarged self-space cannot be sustained by effort, but an effort can be made to enlarge it in such a way that the enlargement can be sustained with ease. Role-playing for a short time is a suitable training procedure. A person who plays the role of a happy man often enough may find himself growing into that role.

Dignity and happiness

Dignity is being happy with oneself. Without that foundation happiness can at best be fleeting pleasure. Dignity is a consciousness of the true self-space. Happiness is the coincidence of self-space and life-space. Dignity is a good foundation for happiness, but happiness (achievement, interests, awareness, sensitivity) can also help dignity by increasing confidence and creating special areas where self-space and life-space more nearly coincide.

Respect is an acknowledgement and valuation of the self-space of oneself, other people and society

In the new meta-system the 'love' of the Christian meta-system is replaced by 'respect'. Love is too much of an emotion. Love blows hot and cold and reverses direction to disappointment and disgust only too easily. Love spans too great a range from intense romantic love to the love one has to feel for an enemy. Love is unreliable and very difficult to produce on demand. Love is so idealistic as a social lubricant that the effort to use it usually ends in failure with the result that no social lubricant is used except mutual inhibition. If we replace love with something that is much easier to use then there is more chance of its being used. It is quite difficult to love an enemy unless you are approaching saintliness – but it is easy to *respect* an enemy.

The shift from love to respect is for the sake of practicality. It is also tied in with the central place given in the new meta-system to self. You can respect the self or self-space of another human being even if you find it possible to love only some of these selves. The shift to respect is not a matter of rejecting love. Love remains an ideal and a bonus. Respect is the foundation. If love can be built on this then so much the better. In fact using respect as the first step can make it easier to move towards love.

Many marriage counsellors would agree that the best marriages are built on mutual respect rather than on love. Respect is durable. Respect acknowledges another person's dignity whereas love often makes demands upon it. Love can be a hunger, a need, a temporary madness, whereas respect is understanding and appreciation.

The three respects

The new meta-system is based on three respects:

respect for oneself, or dignity;
respect for others;
respect for society.

Man is a social animal and this involves interacting with other people. The way he behaves towards other people is as important as the way he behaves towards himself. A man who is happy with himself and has dignity will behave in a dignified manner towards other people. A man who is ill at ease with himself will grasp and struggle in his dealings with other people just as a non-swimmer will thrash about in the water in order to keep himself afloat. That is why man's duty towards his self must often come before his duty towards his fellows – but should never be at the expense of his fellows. In terms of the priority of interests his own self comes first – but when there is a conflict of interests then the consideration of others comes first. This apparent paradox is described in more detail in a later section. The reason is that a man at ease with himself will be at ease with society.

The third respect in the new meta-system is the respect for society. This is respect for the system of society. It is an acknowledgement and an understanding that for social-man to exist in groups there has to be a structure or organization called society. This society is itself an organization just a man is, and society has a 'self' and self-space. Respect is directed towards the self of society. This respect is not for a particular government system and even less for a particular political party. The respect is an acknowledgement that society needs to exist just as personal self needs to exist. It is anti-anarchy. This point will also be elaborated in more detail in a later section. The respect for society is not the type of respect demanded by Marxism in which the interests of the State completely override the interests of the individual. The priority of an individual is always towards his own self, but happiness is not to be achieved at the expense of others or the social system.

Positive respect

The new meta-system puts an emphasis on positive and constructive attitudes. It is not enough to have a list of 'don'ts' and things to be avoided. Life is to be guided not just by a series of warning notices but by positive direction indicators. The pursuit of happiness is one such positive indicator. The pursuit of dignity is a second. The third is the pursuit of respect.

Positive respect sets up certain expectations. It is not just a matter of keeping a cool distance and not interfering. We can respect a crocodile in this way. But we can go further and respect a plant by watering it. Although the new meta-system does put an emphasis on independence of spirit (the self-space must not contain any dependence) the purpose of respect is not to create a society of coolly independent, non-interfering people all minding their own business.

Ordinary interaction

In the course of a day a person comes into contact with a variety of other people: some are friends, others are acquaintances and many are strangers. Respect involves giving each of them attention, self-space and importance as appropriate. Each person has a right to his own self-importance and to have this acknowledged. A person who disregards the importance or dignity of another is failing to provide the required respect.

In a busy shopping street thousands of pedestrians move along the pavements. Although there are thousands of people milling around, very rarely do people actually bump into each other. This is because each person makes an effort not to collide with another and moves so as to allow the other person room for movement. In the same way we can avoid intruding on other people's self-space. The world is full of self-spaces milling around. In general, with a little awareness and sensitivity, we can respect these self-spaces and avoid bumping into them. That is what respect is about: acknowledging the right of a person to his self-space or dignity.

In its positive aspect respect can go further. Where appropriate we can make an effort (which costs us nothing) to increase the self-space and self-importance of others: by smiling at them or greeting them, by listening to what they have to say, by flattering them with regard to matters that are flatterable. Noticing people is part of respecting them. There is, however, a dividing line between positive respect and intrusion. A person may be alone because he wants to be alone and not because he is lonely.

Competition

In the course of dealing with other people there may be many competitive situations: in sport, in business, in love, in art and in politics. Some people enjoy competition and some do not. In Harry Truman's famous words, 'If you don't like the heat, stay out of the kitchen.' The rules of respect apply in competition just as the rules of boxing apply in boxing, or of fencing in fencing. The first rule is that competition is restricted to the area of the competition. In a business competition or a political wrangle dragging in personal history and scandal is irrelevant. The attacking of a person rather than an issue can be justified, for example, in politics, but must be confined to those personal characteristics that are going to be relevant, such as decisiveness, honesty and judgement. The second rule is the avoidance of cheating. Special knowledge is not cheating but dishonesty or deliberate deception is. Where a group or institution has adopted a code of rules because in general the application of the rules is for the benefit of all, a system-cheat can often make headway by disregarding the rules (as for example in the city of London). This aspect of system-cheating is discussed more fully in a later section. The third rule is to respect the other competitors, not just because of their power and skill but because of their selves.

Conflict

There are times when one self-space does bump into another either deliberately or by accident. How does respect deal with this situation? The Christian ethic demanded the turning of the other cheek. What does the new meta-system suggest? The answer is the shrug. Is it really so important? Does it really intrude so much upon one's own self-space? Is not getting upset about it likely to lead to an even greater diminution of self-space?

You are in an hotel and the person next door decides to type out a book. Some of the sound seeps through the walls. You fume and fret, get irritated and complain. You have allowed the noise to enter your life-space as a pressure. You now feel you have to deal with the pressure. The person on the other side of the writer's room just shrugs and fails to notice the sound after a while. He does not fume and fret. He has entered the noise into his self-space and can cope with it.

You are driving along a road, keeping to the speed limit, and some idiot roars past you. You feel annoyed and angry at this show-off and his apparent disregard for other road users. Why? Does his overtaking you diminish your speed? It is true that as a member of the general motoring public you would prefer the road to be free of such dangerous drivers and there would be some point in taking his number and reporting him for dangerous driving, but to regard it as a personal intrusion on your self-space only puts pressure on yourself.

Someone does something which you feel offends or insults you: either deliberately or by omitting to give you the importance you feel is your due. You feel that as a matter of *principle* you have to stand up for your rights. You may even go so far as to fight to avenge the insult to your dignity. There is no harm in fighting if both you and the person you are fighting enjoy that activity, but to do so to avenge your dignity is a contradiction. If your dignity has depended on the approval of others then it is no dignity: the self-space must contain no dependence. So you shrug and as you shrug you no longer feel insulted. Instead of being insulted there is now only a person who is trying to insult you, and such ineffective insulting diminishes that person without bothering you. To respond to an insult or slight is to diminish your dignity as desired by the insulter.

Bullying

There can, however, be a limit to the shrug. Bullying, like system-cheating, is one of the few 'sins' condemned by the new meta-system. Bullying includes the pusher, the smart-alec, the what-you-can-get-away-with merchant. The first response is the shrug. If a bull charges, get out of the way. If a bully derives a pleasure from goading your responses then diminish that pleasure by providing none. The next stage is a calm and steadfast refusal to give way – but this is not on a matter of principle but on matters of fact. This is a sort of passive resistance but a very definite resistance. The third stage is to make quite clear the boundaries of your self-space and to commit yourself in fact and not just in threat to what you intend to do if they are crossed. This is the point for group or combined pressure on a bully. By this time you will probably have made your resistance to the bullying an area of achievement which actually gives you pleasure.

Help

The Christian meta-system includes the idiom of the Good Samaritan who stops to help an injured stranger. This concept of help is an important one, especially in a society where help can often cause considerable trouble and inconvenience to the helper. For example, a man who goes to the aid of someone who is being attacked may end up stabbed himself. How does the concept of respect involve someone in a type of help that is more easily based on compassion? As mentioned before, helping others will always remain one of the most available and satisfying achievement areas. But the main drive must come from the fact that in the new meta-system help for others is part of the social system expectations. It is one of the positive aspects of system respect. Any social system is made up of three elements: organization, rules, and mutual help. The first two cannot take over the function of the third. A person who refuses help has diminished his self-space by failing to cope with an expectaton or demand. You help a person not because you respect that person (though this can also suffice) but because you respect society.

Responsibility

Responsibility involves a status quo in which any change is likely to result in a considerable diminution in the self-space of one of the parties or at least a decrease in the cope/demand ratio through an increase in pressures. It is a difficult area because there are genuine responsibilities and there are also the responsibilities which one party seeks to *impose* upon another in order to shift to that other some of the burden of a life-space (transferring pressures). The same rules of respect apply. An intrusion or diminution of the self-space of another is to be avoided. On the other hand, a self-space should not include such a heavy dependence on someone else. But a person who voluntarily takes over the coping with the life-space of another should be aware of the difficulty of shedding this load. As in so many other areas, it is a matter of balance. The ideal is the independence of self-space.

Size of respect

Respect is the reflection of dignity. A person who has full dignity gets full respect. If the ego in a particular person is much larger than that person's self-space, then respect is accorded to the self-space rather than the ego. Respect is earned, not demanded.

The mood is that of spring – of the beauty of the moment and the positive sense of life opening up

We can now look at the general mood of the new meta-system. The mood concerns the flavour of the system rather than its foundations, structures, concepts and principles. Many of the points listed in this section will have been touched upon in preceding sections and may be taken up again in later sections. There is, however, a usefulness in bringing them together here. The mood outlined in this section may have become obvious to the reader as he read through the preceding sections. Or he may have become bogged down in some problem of detail or even some inconsistency in the proposed meta-system. It should be pointed out here that the system is not intended to be a watertight theological structure. The mood and attitude is more important than the structure. The structure is, however, required to give substance to the mood just as a skeleton gives operating substance to a body, keeping it from being a floppy mass of flesh. The structure is not a restricting one but a liberating one. A cage is a restricting structure but a ladder is an operating one: it allows us to do more easily what might have been difficult without it.

Holiday mood

Life is regarded as a holiday from non-existence. The wonderful system of man has come together as a system and its function is to function as man. The holiday mood includes enjoyment and the pursuit of happiness both in activity and also in awareness and appreciation. There is tolerance and relaxation. On holiday there are not the fixed expectations and pressures that are left behind at home. There is a willingness to take what comes. There is also an eagerness to get on with other people. Most people are at their best on holiday.

Other beliefs

There is no quarrel with any other belief system. Indeed it will be claimed that many of the principles suggested here are, or were, implicit in many of these. The new meta-system can *coexist* with any other belief system that does not demand intolerance. Although the mood has been described as being a holiday from non-existence, this can as easily apply to being a holiday between non-existence and the next world, if that is part of the belief system. I do not believe that there is any belief system that would positively make *unhappiness* in this world a necessity for entering the next one. Most belief systems seek to make this world at least tolerable when faced through the perceptual framework of the belief.

Positive

The attitude is positive. This means a focusing on the positive aspects of life and on the positive aspects of man's nature. Man is not a saint or even always a lovable sinner, but there is no intrinsic design in the system of man that inclines him towards evil. The emphasis is on the positive, life-enhancing aspects of existence, whether they happen or whether they need to be sought out or cultivated.

The emphasis is shifted from the negative, carping, critical role of mind to the expanding, positive role. It is a matter of building on what is good rather than complaining at what is bad. Building is acknowledged as a better way of creating than is destruction.

Constructive

Bringing things about and making things happen have a higher importance than opposition. Direction and cause are to be obtained by constructive change and alternatives rather than by constant opposition. Opposition has its place but not as a creative or constructive force – more as a modifier or regulator. Dialectic polemic and debate are replaced by the more constructive *exlectic* process. Constructiveness is regarded as being the combination of creativity with effectiveness.

Happiness and enjoyment

The pursuit of happiness and enjoyment is the legitimate purpose of life (as is recognized by the constitution of the United States of America). No one can be guaranteed happiness – and no one can demand that someone else supply him with it. But he himself has the right and the duty to pursue it in whichever form suits his talents and abilities. The one proviso is that it must not be obtained at the expense of others or at the expense of society. A happy man is a fulfilled man.

Self

The self is very important. Self-care has priority of consideration over all other cares – but not necessarily priority in a conflict of interests. Man is to enjoy, value and respect his self. Dignity is the point at which self-love is the same as happiness. Dignity is regarded as a better protection against selfishness than is self-denial. A happy self is looked to as the basis of a happy society. A man who is not at ease with himself is unlikely to be at ease with other people or society. Self-interest and self-importance are to be encouraged to the point of dignity: beyond that they become counter-effective.

Respect

Respect is a quiet acknowledgement of the existence and the rights of oneself, of others and of society. Respect is to be an understanding of the human system. Respect is to be the foundation upon which happiness can be built. Respect is vision that is both clear and positive.

Humour

There is a sense of tolerance and a sense of proportion. There is an absence of agony, frenzy and intensity. It is the smile of humour rather than the guffaw. Humour is a protection against the solemnity and over-seriousness that can so easily become an emotional cage. Humour is an acceptance of different ways of looking at life and a reminder of the ever-present possibility of being able to look at things in a new way.

Tolerance

Tolerance is a key element. It arises from humour and from proto-truth and from a respect for others. It is a tolerance of different views, of different roles, of different personalities. It is a tolerance of everything except intolerance. It is not a passive, apathetic tolerance but an active tolerance of understanding. Tolerance includes the shrug and the smile where otherwise a conflict might have developed.

Plurality

There is room for a plurality of moods, of people, of routes to happiness. There is no urging towards a single state of ultimate perfection and the ideal man. Each person is his own ideal. Dignity is valued not as to its content but as to its ease. Plurality avoids polarization by including extremes instead of forcing them apart. Plurality avoids dissent by accepting the intrinsic validity of a different point of view. But plurality is not the passivity of any-thing-goes: it is an appreciation of variety and individuality.

Gentle

The mood of the new meta-system is gentle and low-key. There is no emphasis on fervour or enthusiasm or the necessity for belief. But it is the gentleness of strength, not of weakness – in the way only powerful pianists can play the gentle passages with full control. Fierceness is self-consuming and disruptive: blind rage is blind, especially when it is headed purposefully in the wrong direction.

Sensitivity

Sensitivity and responsiveness are important because they provide the basis for both happiness and respect. The deliberate search for happiness may well require an increase in sensitivity. But sensitivity should not be pursued as an end in itself because that can become counter-effective and destroy the robust ability of a person to survive in a complex society. Pursued as an end in itself, sensitivity can double the pressures on an individual and in no way help him to overcome them. Private hells are more often created by misplaced sensitivity than by circumstance. Nor should sensitivity be encouraged to the point of self-indulgence where all activity is directed inwards.

Effectiveness

This is an important aspect of the new meta-system. Man is to value effectiveness in himself and in others. Effectiveness is the proper functioning of a system whatever its nature. Effectiveness is an *operating principle* that gives a value to whatever is being done. If something is being done then it is worth doing effectively. Effectiveness is to an action what dignity is to a person.

Focus

The mind is to be capable of being focused in a deliberate manner. Focus is the opposite of drift. Man is to have a *definite* – but not rigid – sense of himself and of the world around him. Focus is the opposite of a pebble on the beach that washes in and out at the dictate of the waves. If it was man's destiny to be inanimate, then it is a waste that he should be endowed with animation. Animation includes deliberation and focus. Life is not to be treated as an amorphous wave of incomprehensibility. There are things to be looked at, things to be enjoyed and things to be done provided one can focus on them instead of being submerged by totality.

Activity

There is to be activity, directed both inwards and outwards. Activity is being alive and being lively. Activity is the opposite of passivity, drift, resignation and *ennui*. Activity is thinking with muscles as surely as thinking is activity without them. Activity is no way inferior to thought. Activity has its own value. Activity is a major route to happiness.

Achievement

There is the achievement of performance as well as the achievement of destination. The achievement of performance is more important and more surely a means to happiness. Achievement is the definition of the self in action. Life itself is the achievement of a self-organizing system, and living is its achievement of performance. Achievement is personal and is to be carefully distinguished from the image of high-achievement pressure and the competitive need. A carpenter is a more successful achiever than a politician.

Involvement

Involvement is the opposite of apathy. The framework of importance includes society, the community and oneself. Within that framework everything is of importance and worthy of involvement. Involvement is activity and achievement. Apathy is self-denial. An apathetic person is someone who is insufficiently fuelled by self.

System sins

Because the emphasis of the new meta-system is on the positive and constructive side there are relatively few 'sins'. In broad terms (that will be explored more fully later) the sins include the following. Self-abdication to drugs, doctrines or anything else; self and self-care are central to the new meta-system. System-parasites and system-cheats show a respect for the system but live off other people's willingness to make it work. Bullying shows a lack of respect for the self-space of others. Passivity and apathy are anti-life. Negativity, sneers and destructiveness are anti-happiness.

Control

Man is in control of his destiny or at least of his self and his happiness. The self should contain no dependence on others. Through activity or the changing of his perceptions man creates and controls the perceptual world in which he lives. Man has only himself to blame for his unhappiness.

Practical and realistic

The mood of the new meta-system is practical and realistic. There is no attempt to urge people towards perfection or to the attainment of impossible ideals. There are no absolutes and infinities. Ordinary people and ordinary life are what matter. The guidelines are flexible like a tree that gives a little in a high wind. There may well be exceptional circumstances that make it difficult to apply many of the suggestions or even render them invalid. But the suggestions apply to the broad average of situations and they remain suggestions. As with water, there is fluidity and flexibility, but in its way water is real and definite.

Opportunity

The world is to be regarded as an opportunity for happiness, not a burden to be endured. Individual situations are to be regarded as full of opportunity rather than full of threatening pressures. Seeking out the opportunities or making the perceptual change necessary may require effort, but that is part of the activity of life. On the other hand, no one should be bullied by opportunity, bullied by the need to make the best possible choice, bullied by the need to get the best possible deal. There has to be the practical application of trade-offs and cut-offs. No one can do everything or know everything or be perfect.

Day-to-day

The meta-system is concerned with day-to-day life rather than with great enterprises. It is concerned with moment-to-moment life rather than the rituals of church celebration. A person can move in and out of the meta-system as often as he wishes; even several times a day. Life is lived in small things and it is around these that happiness must be built rather than on a hoped-for future. Now-care is as important as future-care – or more important.

Balance

Balance is extremely important and will be discussed more fully in a later section. There is to be balance between extremes. There is to be balance in the attention paid to different things. There is to be balance in a mix which has different ingredients. There is balance between the inner world and the outer world. There is balance between now-care and future-care. There is balance between adjusting to the circumstances or changing them. There is balance between activity and awareness. Balance can be difficult but it is better consciously to face that difficulty than to abolish it by abolishing the things on which it depends.

Wisdom

The emphasis is quite definitely on wisdom rather than cleverness. Wisdom is a matter of *perception*: of looking at the world and oneself. Intellectual games and intellectual achievement, like other games and achievement, are for those who find pleasure in them.

Simplicity

Simplicity and directness are the operating idiom of the new meta-system.

The new meta-system could be said to be based on the nature of perception and the pursuit of happiness

Having looked in the preceding section at the general mood of the new meta-system, we can summarize the structure of the system before we move on to consider in the following pages the *application* of the meta-system to daily life.

Belief

The new meta-system is not derived from or dependent upon a particular set of beliefs. As a working background it is assumed that man is a functioning biological system who usually lives in an organizational system called society. The meta-system *requires* no explanation of man's origins or destiny. An explanation of man's origins may, however, be found in the behaviour of self-organizing systems and the self-organization of basic chemicals into higher and higher orders of organization until man is the culmination.

The emphasis is on the here and now rather than on some after-life or release from the cycle of life. The purpose of the human system is identified as the proper functioning of the human system, and this is defined as happiness. The pursuit of happiness therefore becomes the main purpose of life.

Man's mind

Man's mind creates the world in which he lives. Man lives according to his own map of the world, his own way of seeing things, which has been created by his perception. The process of perception is a self-organizing one in which signals from the external world received through the senses are converted into nerve excitations in the brain. These excitations organize themselves into recorded patterns. The patterns are individual and depend on circumstances, past experience and the particular sequence of arrival of the information. It is quite possible for the same information to be put together in another pattern by a different brain or by the same brain in the process known as insight or creativity.

Lateral thinking is a provocative process used for changing the patterns of perception. Thinking, in general, is an exploration of the map of the world created by perception. The purpose of thinking is either direct enjoyment or else a change in the world map intended to increase happiness. This change in the world map may take the form of an adjustment to circumstances or an alteration of circumstances by means of activity which follows the thinking. The balance between adjustment of oneself or alteration of circumstances is emphasized.

Proto-truths

The new system replaces absolute truth with proto-truth. Absolute truths only exist in circular systems or special universes. Proto-truths exist in the sort of open universe with which science and life deal. A proto-truth is as free from conscious error or deception as any other truth, but it is never held to be unchangeable. A proto-truth is believable so long as it is realized that it can be improved or replaced by a better one.

Proto-truths are regarded as relatively stable states in the evolution of ideas. The self-organization of experience forms such stable states both in the mind of individuals and also in society as a whole. There are individual proto-truths or cultural proto-truths. Proto-truths are not dogmas but acceptable and sensible ways of looking at the world that fit experience. Proto-truths may be changed by new experience or by the restructuring of existing experience.

Because proto-truths are not regarded as absolute there is no effort to impose them on other people, and this gives rise to the tolerance of the new meta-system. Nor is there a need to defend the proto-truths at all costs, and this gives rise to the positive and constructive attitude of the meta-system. Improvement in the proto-truths is brought about by the process of exlectics instead of dialectics. Dialectics seek improvement by a process of *attack* and clash whereas exlectics seek improvement by *reconstruction* of the initial idea.

Biodic symbol

The main track and the side track of the biodic symbol refer to the possibility of changing patterns in a patterning system such as perception. The symbol therefore symbolizes perception, change, possibility and hope. It symbolizes the possibility of escaping from a particular way of looking at things.

Humour is a key element in the new meta-system because it is the characteristic of mind that arises directly from the biodic process. Humour indicates a switch in patterns: a sudden change to a different way of looking at things. Humour is also tolerant, easy-going and good-natured.

Self

The new meta-system is definitely *self-centred*. Instead of denying the self, as do so many religious meta-systems, the new meta-system places self at the centre of concern. Man's first priority of consideration (though not necessarily in a conflict of interests) is his self. If a man is at ease with himself then he will be at ease with the world and he will be happy.

Life-space

Life-space refers to the total pressures, demands and expectations that are made upon an individual by himself, by others and by circumstances. For this reason life-space may also be called *demand-space*. Life-space is also the space in which an individual will be operating – to meet the pressures and expectations. So life-space may be called the operating-space.

Self-space

Self-space is that part of the life-space with which a person can cope with ease. Self-space can also be called *cope-space*. Cope-space or self-space includes that part of the demand-space that a man has as it were 'under control' or 'under his skin'. Within his self-space man must be his own master. The self-space may be affected by outside influences but must not depend on some outside thing or person for its functioning. When a person is within his self-space he is free and independent.

Cope/demand ratio

When self-space enlarges to coincide with life-space that is happiness. The usual gap between the two is the opportunity-space or the pressure-space, depending on how it is seen by the individual. An unfulfilled opportunity is, however, a pressure of sorts. The cope/demand ratio refers to the amount of life-space that is filled by self-space. If self-space completely fills life-space the ratio is unity. If self-space only half fills life-space the ratio is one half. If self-space fills only one quarter of the life-space the ratio is one quarter. An increase in the cope/demand ratio (for example, from one quarter to one half) means either that the self-space has increased or that the life-space has shrunk – and it signifies a move towards happiness.

Dignity

The ego refers to a person's self-image or the image which he wants others to have of himself. When the ego corresponds exactly to the self-space then there is dignity. Dignity is the destination for the self. When a man has dignity he is at ease with himself. When a man has dignity he can respect himself. The degree of dignity is determined not by the content of the self-space but by the closeness of fit of ego and self-space.

Respect

Respect replaces love as the operating idiom of the meta-system on the basis that respect is more workable. There are three basic respects: respect of an individual for himself; respect of an individual for others; respect of an individual for society.

Happiness

The pursuit of happiness is the legitimate purpose of the human system. Happiness is based on enjoyment of the self and dignity. Happiness includes ingredients that can become counter-effective unless used with care and balance. These include pleasure, excitement and enthusiasm. There are other, more dependable, ingredients such as peace, joy, interest and achievement.

Activity

Activity is important and so is involvement. Activity can be directed inwards at the internal world or outwards at the external world. There can be the activity of *action* or the activity of *awareness*. Activity involves achievement: the achievement of destination or the more preferable achievement of performance. Activity is of value because it enlarges the self-space.

Key elements

The key elements can be summarized as perception, humour, self, dignity, respect and happiness.

Part Two
Application

*Man is ultimately in control of the inner world formed by his per-
ception of the outer world*

The following sections will deal with the application of the new
meta-system. Application involves mood and attitude, strategy
and principles. Some people require matters to be spelt out in
detail. Others prefer to be given broad principles which they themselves can work into strategies.

The meta-system can put an emphasis on self and on happiness
and can encourage people to do likewise with their own lives. This
can serve two purposes. It can overcome people's inhibitions about
paying attention to self and happiness if this has been discouraged
in the past. It can also offer them a goal towards which people can
move in their own way. It is not possible to spell out in detail a
path or procedure that will guarantee dignity or happiness. But it
is possible to indicate the sort of things that will increase the
possibility. If you throw a pair of dice you cannot determine
which numbers will come up. But if you do not even attempt to
throw a pair of dice then you can be sure that *no* numbers will
come up. Moreover, if you decide to be satisfied by alternative
pairs of numbers, then this decision of yours will make it easier for
you to be satisfied even though you still cannot guarantee success.

Life is like playing tennis. There is no formula for winning but
there is room for the development of a definite skill that will make
happiness more likely. You can get better at tennis and you can
practise different strokes. Happiness can be treated in the same
way.

The meta-system offers a framework for looking at things, for putting things together. For instance, it can be seen that the problem of self can be treated in a way different from that of the self-denial insisted upon by some religious meta-systems. The concept of a proto-truth can solve the problems created by an insistence on absolute truth. The process of exlectics can lead to a tackling of problems in a new way.

It is not just a matter of moving in the right direction: as the biodic symbol suggests, it may be a matter of *stopping* moving in a wrong direction. We may need to go back and change concepts rather than use the old ones more fervently.

The preference is for what is life-enhancing over what is life-cramping

Hindus do not define God. Instead they list all the things which he is not. Animals flee from a forest fire, their direction determined only by what they are fleeing from. A swimmer uses the end of the swimming pool in order to push off in a new direction. The attitudes listed in this section are not meant to be 'sins' to be avoided, because anyone who was guilty of them would never admit to the guilt. Instead they are attitudes to flee from or to push off from. With honesty one may notice them in oneself – on occasions or as a life style. It may be easier to notice them in other people and by observing them determine to avoid them. Imagine that someone is observing you even as you observe them.

To some extent the attitudes listed here are the negative image of the atittudes listed in the mood section. That is inevitable. For example, the attitudes listed there were positive and life-enhancing whereas those listed here are negative and *life-cramping*.

In practical terms, on a day-to-day basis, and as a start in the use of the new meta-system, it is easier to know what to move away from than what to move towards, since the latter is less tangible. In practice one may catch oneself falling into the trap of one of these attitudes and by noticing this – and without feeling any guilt – build up an aversion to negativity.

Negativity

In most situations it is much easier to pick out the faults because these are more obvious since they are based on what we think a thing should be. That is to say, being negative is based on our past experience whereas being positive requires us to look into the future to assess something new. A man who designs a new dress is likely to be told that it is old-fashioned because a comparison with the past is always possible – to assess the dress's virtues requires more effort. Anything new seems to involve effort, therefore it is easier to be negative.

Criticism

Negative criticism is easy because it is always possible to find fault with anything if one looks hard enough. It is quite easy to concentrate on the faults and ignore what is worth-while. But the main and overriding attraction of criticism is that it at once makes the critic superior to what he is criticizing. A man who criticizes a play implies that he has seen better plays and that he knows what a better play is like. A girl who criticizes a party wants people to know that she is used to going to better parties. A book critic wants his readers to know that *he* has not been taken in. Praise, on the other hand, seems to imply subservience and naïvety. If one person praises a restaurant and another criticizes it then the critic feels that she knows what good food is really like whereas the praiser is satisfied with any old thing. Because criticism is so easy it is often the refuge of mediocre minds who cannot be interesting in any other way. Too often a critic forgets that he is not criticizing the situation but only his understanding of it. A book critic may be indicating his lack of understanding of the book as much as its deficiencies. In practice you do not have to understand something to criticize it – indeed, criticism is very often a camouflage for lack of understanding.

Opposition

There are those who derive their vigour, mission and direction in life only from opposition and complaint. There are those who believe that improvement can only come about through clash. There are those who feel that any discussion should become a polarized argument. There are those who feel that all situations are battles in which one side loses and the other side gains. There are those who feel that their egos depend on battling and winning.

Put-downs

As a variant of criticism there is the put-down which involves the pushing down of someone else in order to obtain a feeling of superiority. There are those who feel that the most palpable gain must be at someone else's expense. This may be due to a perversion of the competitive spirit or just socialized aggression. It may also be the expression of weakness that fears discovery and has therefore to strike first. It may also, innocently, be a vehicle for wit.

Sneer

A sneer is too easy. All it requires is that you have within earshot someone similarly affected with jealousy. To sneer you choose your frame of reference to fit the judgement you wish to make. Language has an ample supply of words to suit a sneer. If a girl is well dressed she is prissy or pretentious. If she is badly dressed she is a slob. If she is neutrally dressed she is nondescript or mousy. A sneer has no social value whatsoever except to self-label the impotent.

Superiority

The élitist, the snob, the holier-than-thou, the cleverer-than-thou may well have genuine grounds for their feeling of superiority. There are people who are cleverer and holier than others just as there are people who are richer than others. Is it possible that the flaunting of these superiorities is no more than an enjoyment of them? If so why should anyone else mind? What is resented is the implication that because a person is superior along some dimension he is *generally* superior. This is a special form of egotism and pretension. A properly fitting ego would evoke respect and even admiration rather than resentment.

Pretension

A pretension is a make-believe act both for the person offering it and for those towards whom it is directed. Unfortunately only one of the parties usually knows this. True style and eccentricity are not pretension but a genuine ego and self-space fit. The usual sort of pretension is an ego too large for its self-space – with the obvious lack of dignity as a result.

Egotism

It may seem strange that a meta-system that places so much emphasis on the self and self-care should regard egotism as something to be avoided. It must be obvious, however, that egotism is the opposite of dignity. Dignity is when ego and self-space coincide. Egotism is when the ego is much larger than the self-space and can therefore only be sustained by a demand on the approval of others. We do expect false modesty as a social gesture from those whose self-spaces may be large enough to support large egos, but we have no right to expect it except the right of jealousy.

Bullying

This is the derivation of pleasure or achievement directly at the expense of another. It is a parody of the stag or bull who fights the strongest in the herd in order to establish his superiority. Bullying is a totally unnecessary intrusion into someone else's life-space in order to enlarge one's own self-space. Bullying goes against the basis of respect and as a result a bully forfeits respect.

What you can get away with

This is the system-cheat or parasite who operates an ethic completely devoid of respect and considers himself smart on that account. He is a man who feels that only fear makes people obey the requirements of the system, and since he believes himself too smart for fear he despises those who seem to show it. It never occurs to the system-cheat that a system is only operable if those using it respect it in terms of acknowledging the need for it to function.

Violence

The display of rage or force in order to achieve an end is a combination of bullying and the system-cheat. Those who derive pleasure from violence place too high an emphasis on excitement. Just as a crime involving violence tends to be a badly thought-out crime, so violence is an alternative to thought.

Cynicism

Beneath the face lies the skull. It is usually possible to look for, and find, an explanation of something that will fit a prejudice. The cynic believes himself to be a realist, but a realism that destroys values is too negative to be worth having. As Oscar Wilde put it, a cynic is someone who knows the price of everything and the value of nothing. Cynicism is rampant negativity.

World-weariness

The world-weary, know-it-all, lived-out individual has usually done everything and enjoyed nothing. A person who 'knows' all there is to know and has done all there is to do can only be a myopic mental cripple. A world-weary person is someone who has relied entirely on excitement and pleasure and has proved them to be counter-effective.

Boredom

Boredom is the hallmark of a taker: someone who has invested nothing in happiness but insists on a right to be excited and entertained. Most people are bored from time to time and it is unrealistic to expect otherwise, but a person who declares himself to be habitually bored with life is either a poseur or sleep-walking.

Apathy

Apathy is the most anti-life of all the attitudes and yet the most understandable. If a person has no hope and no feeling of control, then apathy is but the soothing of despair. A person who is apathetic has given up trying because all problems seem insoluble. Yet there must be some small area of achievement on which it is possible to *build*. Apathy is an opting out of life.

Drift

Unlike apathy, drift is more a matter of laziness – of refusal to make any investment in life. Drift takes care of the need to make decisions. Drift precludes the possibility of making a mistake. A certain amount of drift is useful to open up possibilities that could not have been planned. A drifting through circumstances may be the deliberate choice of an individual and therefore his right. A drift of spirit or self is a form of self-abdication.

Self-pity

There are few people who do not have cause for self-pity at some time in their lives. But it is neither consoling nor effective. It tends to be an indulgence which grows upon itself until it precludes action and makes ever-increasing demands on other people. One has only to see the different susceptibilities of people to self-pity to realize that it arises more from the self than from circumstances. It is a form of egotism.

Props

The use of drugs, alcohol and other props for the self is a direct form of self-abdication. The self is unlikely to develop unless it is given a chance to do so. Such props are usually an attempt to shrink life-space to manageable proportions or to obtain ecstasy without effort.

Passivity

A person who is not prepared to do anything on his own behalf denies his self and his being alive. A person who is passive is badly in need of the new meta-system. There has to be a will to do something, no matter how ineffectively it may operate.

Thinking is the tool with which man appreciates, explores and changes the inner world and plans the actions that can change the outer world

Thinking plays a central role in the new meta-system because it is the tool with which the mind can act both on the inner world of perception and on the external world through action. The two processes of adjustment and change have an origin in thinking. Thinking of the high-powered intellectual sort is not required. Wisdom is much more important than intelligence. None of the problems are difficult to solve. What is required is a consciousness of thinking as the tool of mind and a confidence and enjoyment in its use. Being wrong is not important so long as there is no arrogance. Like the exhaust gases from a motor car, being wrong now and then indicates that thinking is taking place and not just ego-prancing.

The purpose of thinking

The purpose of thinking can be listed under the following headings.

Enjoyment The exploration of experience for pleasure – nostalgia, day-dreams, reveries, reading, passive entertainment, the exploration of an interesting subject and in general the pleasures of exploration of the past or the present. Thinking is a perfectly legitimate source of pleasure, quite apart from playing chess or doing crossword puzzles. Those who dislike thinking do so because they equate it with frustratingly difficult situations or the ego-involvement of argument or intellectual gymnastics.

Problem-solving Bringing something about. Most thinking situations can be put in terms of a 'problem'. If there is a desire to bring something about (solve the problems created by inflation, or design a new toy) then thinking can be applied in a problem-solving way. The definition of the problem can make a difference to the ease with which it is solved.

Review Audits and an examination and mapping of the status quo. This is a descriptive use of thinking which may be directed inwards or outwards. It may involve simplification and clarification. When directed inwards it requires objectivity and honesty. The descriptive use of thinking is the only one taught in schools, and that is only outward directed description. In the new meta-system inward directed description and auditing are important.

Perceptual change A deliberate attempt to change not the world but the way we are looking at it. This usually involves lateral thinking. Perceptual change is the basic tool of adjustment. It may also be of value in problem-solving.

These are broad categories of purpose and there is considerable overlap. For example, review and understanding can be part of enjoyment and also part of problem-solving. Perceptual change can be part of problem-solving and problem-solving can be part of perceptual change.

Starting-point

The starting-point for thinking is always an exploration of the inner world created by perception. The perception may be of something which is immediately present (but we only understand it in terms of experience) or of matters which are not present at the moment (like financial planning or budgeting). The main problem here is one of drift. People wait for ideas to come into their minds and then drift from point to point. The examination of each point may be excellent, but the points are only an arbitrary sample of the whole situation. If you rely on one point to generate the next one you will have the characteristic point-to-point thinking of young children. To avoid this there is a need for a definite framework of attention which includes scan, focus and analysis.

Scan   This involves a deliberate framework for carrying attention over the whole field. This broad perspective does not happen naturally, but is essential for effective thinking. All the factors have to be taken into consideration – it is not worth buying a car that does not fit your garage. Can also include a process of mapping. For example, in a conflict situation both sides could cooperate to produce a map of the conflict area showing the areas of agreement, and the areas that were agreed to be irrelevant. There could then be a reaction to this map instead of the usual polemical confrontation.

Focus   The ability to focus directly and purposefully on some aspect of the situation. This is much more difficult than it seems, and most thinkers only have a general idea of what they are thinking about. Focus is not the same as identification of the problem. It is the deliberate isolation of a small part of the general situation. With comparison, judgement, assessment of priorities and other such situations it may be necessary to hold different things in focus or at least to be able to switch back and forth from one focus to another.

Analysis   An analysis turns a focal point into a whole field by looking in detail at what has been focused upon and breaking it down into even smaller areas each of which can become a point of focus. Analysis is particularly useful in overcoming the problems created by the 'lump effect' in which attention is paid to a word or concept that includes several sub-concepts. It must be emphasized that analysis is by no means the whole of thinking, and analysis by itself will not solve problems. In the past rather too much attention has been paid to logical analysis as the only required tool of thinking.

Framework

The two biggest problems with the initial or starting point of thinking are *confusion* and *drift*. Both can be overcome by the application of an artificial and external framework. The framework allows the thinker to direct his attention to one area after another instead of trying to deal with everything at once. The framework sets up a sequence of stages and allows the thinker to concentrate on each stage in succession. One such framework is used in the CoRT Thinking programme (CoRT stands for Cognitive Research Trust).* This is the TEC-PISCO framework and is made up as follows:

Target (T): focus directly on some target.

Expand (E): expand and elaborate and say as much as you can about the target including the creation of alternatives. Expansion in depth and in breadth.

Contract (C): extract the important point, narrow down, come to a decision or conclusion.

This TEC process is a general framework tool that can then be applied during any one of the actual problem-solving stages of the PISCO process, which is made up as follows:

Purpose (P): definition of the objective or purpose of the thinking, the end-point that is desired.

Input (I): all the information, factors, considerations that have to be taken into account. Background situation, surrounding situation and future situation are included here.

Solutions (S): alternative solutions to the problem. If there is a 'sticking-point' in the way of a solution, this can be defined as a new problem in itself and tackled with the whole process.

Choice (C): decision and conclusion. Judgement, priorities,

* *CoRT Thinking: Action* (Direct Education Services, Blandford, Dorset, UK).

evaluation criteria are applied in order to choose one from amongst the alternative solutions.

Operation (O): the steps required to put the solution into operation. Thinking does not end with a solution but with a way of putting that solution into action. There needs to be a plan of action.

The above framework is only an example of the sort of framework that can be used to avoid confusion. It happens to be the one that is used in an extensive programme for teaching thinking as a skill in schools.* Such a framework is not a restricting structure but a liberating one because it frees the thinker to think within each area instead of having to keep everything in mind at once.

Being wrong

No one is ever wrong on purpose, but in general the following seem to be the most common faults in thinking.

Instant judgement This includes prejudice. An instant judgement is either brought to the situation or is made from a preliminary glimpse. Thinking is then used not to explore the situation but *solely to support* the conclusion that has already been made. This is a fault that is obvious in politicians, but it is also very common in academics and other clever people who use their thinking as a means of support for their egos rather than as an exploration. Unfortunately it is also what many pupils are taught in school in essay-writing or in debates.

Inadequate scan This means thinking or arguing from only part of the total situation. This is by far the *most common fault* in any thinking anywhere. Obviously no one can know all the information or see all the field, but the deliberate selection of only a small part of the field is inexcusable. By carefully choosing only

* *Teaching Thinking*, Maurice Temple Smith, 1976; Penguin Books, 1979.

part of the situation and deliberately ignoring other parts, a thinker can construct a perfectly logical argument and then rest his case on the logicality of that argument. A person who starts out with a negative attitude of mind will concentrate on those features which are capable of being attacked. This inadequate scan or 'partialism' is of course the basis of our hallowed dialectic process.

Magnitude effect　This involves a train of cause and effect where the magnitudes involved are quite inappropriate. The magnitude effect may be seen in remarks such as: 'A great deal of money could be saved if the social security system was tightened up so that there were fewer cheats.' This sort of remark would follow a newspaper revelation that someone had cheated the system out of £30,000 over two years. Yet in proportion to the total amount of money going through the system this is insignificant. Another remark might be: 'British Industry would have no problems if strikes were made illegal.' In fact the number of working days lost through strikes is very much less than the number lost through minor illnesses. As usual in the magnitude error the effect is going in the right direction but the size of the effect is neglected. Another example might be: 'We must preserve the stock exchange because it is an efficient means of supplying industry with the money it needs.' Certainly the stock exchange does this efficiently but in fact no more than 3 per cent of the finance required by industry is raised by the stock exchange. 'There would be enough to go round if some people did not make excessive profits' is a commonly heard remark. Yet if inflation is taken into account many industries are running at a loss and not even generating enough money to maintain their working capital. There may well be a small number of profiteers especially in such areas as property speculation but this must be set against the whole of industry.

Point-to-point　Here the mind follows along an apparently logical connection, but this is usually based on a very limited view of the situation. For example, it may be argued that since the moon affects the tides and since the human body is over 90 per cent water then it is likely that the stars should affect human destiny.

Point-to-point argument consists of a series of jumps of this sort and has been much used in the past for political and religious purposes.

Being right

Being right is the point of satisfaction at which we 'rest' our thinking. There are various ways of being right. Being right is almost an emotion (just as is the 'rightness' of belief), and this emotion can be based on some of the following circumstances.

Error-free An absence of logical error as perceived by oneself or by an opponent. There seems to be a fit, or the thing seems to 'click' together with a sense of satisfaction and rightness. The belief that error-free thinking is necessarily valid has been by far our biggest cultural block to effective thinking. This is because it has put all the emphasis on logical processing rather than perceptual adequacy. Error-free thinking based on inadequate perception may be dangerously misleading.

Emotional rightness The thinking has done nothing except provide a framework of respectability around emotions that were there all the time. In this type of thinking we are apt to use value-laden words which prejudge the issue. We refer in contempt to 'cow-like' contentment if we wish to argue against contentment.

Unique rightness We feel that the solution we have found is the only possible one. Outside of mathematics where a 'right' answer is a right answer there is no reason to suppose that the first solution found is the only one or indeed the best one. Nor is there any reason to suppose that our solution is any better than someone else's. Unique rightness is based on our *personal* inability to see or even imagine any other solution or explanation. In descriptive sciences like anthropology proof is often no more than lack of imagination. Unique rightness also gives rise to arrogance which is of course the enemy of all thinking and totally inappropriate when we are dealing with proto-truths.

The above idioms of thinking, which are described more fully elsewhere,* need to be kept in mind both with regard to our own thinking and also with regard to the thinking of others.

Decision

Decision is a very important part of thinking, and it is the aspect of thinking that is lacking in the descriptive thinking taught in schools. Much of the thinking in real life has to end, some time, with a decision, because action is based on decision. It may be a decision to do the easiest thing or it may be a decision to make no decision or a definite decision to do nothing (just avoiding a decision is a definite decision *to do nothing* even if it does not seem so).

No decision is perfect. Most decisions have to be based on inadequate knowledge and some guesswork. In particular it is very difficult to know what will happen in the future, and most decisions affect the future.

Decisions are always emotional in the end. *And so they should be.* Ultimately it must be the feelings of the person making the decision that matter most. The purpose of thinking is so to arrange the situation that the emotional decision is the right one. Aids to the rearrangement include the following:

Priorities The thinker draws up a list of priorities and evaluation criteria and then sees which of the alternatives best fit the requirements. This is not as easy as it seems because no alternative will score in one area while another scores elsewhere, and simply adding up the scores usually does not work. It is best to reduce the priorities to just one or two and to add to them the reason, or pressure, for making the decision. Then you see which alternative comes out best.

Review Imagine you had chosen one of the alternatives, and then describe to yourself, in words or on paper, just why you

* *Practical Thinking*, Penguin Books, 1976.

made that decision. See if it seems plausible. Usually it will not. If you can describe in advance, with honesty and with conviction, the reasons for a decision, you will probably not regret it. You may be surprised how often a very appealing choice turns out to be feebly supported by reasons. Do this for each of the alternatives.

Consequences Imagine you have chosen one or other of the alternatives. Draw up a list of plus consequences and minus consequences and also include an area of 'don't knows'. This focus on consequences may make the decision easier because decisions are more often based on how something looks at the moment rather than in the future.

Alteration In order to find out just why an alternative appeals emotionally, make a slight alteration to it. For example, if you have a holiday choice of a particular place you might say: 'Suppose I went there and did not meet anyone new?' You may find that the appeal of the place suddenly vanishes. In that case you have identified the source of the appeal rather than leaving it embedded in the general choice. This is a powerful way of examining the emotional content of alternatives.

There is a psychologically recognized process known as 'cognitive dissonance' which states that a decision will become more attractive after it has been made than before. This protects the decision-maker. If a decision is very evenly balanced, then the toss of a coin should decide it. In practice this can be used. It does not seem very satisfactory because one tends to concentrate on the alternative *that is being given up* and is reluctant to abandon the potentiality of enjoying it as well. In most cases it is this reluctance to give something up that creates difficulty with a decision. A girl undecided between two suitors knows she would be happy with either – but is reluctant to give up the advantages peculiar to either of them. It makes decisions much easier if the thinker concentrates on what he is prepared to give up or 'trade-off' in such a situation.

Lateral thinking

The need for lateral thinking arises directly from the patterning nature of perception. Lateral thinking is concerned with changing perceptions, changing patterns and changing concepts. Instead of building on a particular way of looking at things you move 'sideways' and try to change that perception. By its very nature a patterning system requires a procedure for changing patterns, otherwise the same patterns will be used over again: patterns determine perception, but as we look through the patterns what we see confirms them. It is true that patterns can be changed by mistake and by chance, but that is a slow and unpredictable process. Lateral thinking is the deliberate type of thinking concerned with pattern-changing.

At first sight lateral thinking appears illogical. For example, you may use a completely random input or you may use as a stepping-stone a statement which is quite wrong. Logic demands that what is said must be consistent with and deducible from what has gone before. But the process of lateral thinking is provocation. If what is said is logically consistent with what has gone before, then the established pattern is being used and no provocation is taking place. We do, however, need *a language indicator* to show that a statement is being made as a provocation and not as a statement consistent with experience. The language indicator is the new word 'po' which is explained in detail in *PO: Beyond Yes and No.** It is derived from hypothesis, suppose, possible, and poetry, for in all these situations ideas are used in a provocative manner.

The basic process of lateral thinking is to make a provocative step which takes us out of the main channel we would otherwise have remained within. We now proceed, quite logically, from the new position and see if we can journey to a useful new idea.

The three basic processes of lateral thinking are related to the biodic symbol. They are all designed to increase our chances of

---

* Penguin Books, 1974; Simon & Schuster, New York, 1974.

reaching the 'insight point'. Once we have arrived there it is easy, with *hindsight*, to see the side track that led there all the time. So we use a provocative method to get to the new idea but then prove its value by the side track since the provocative step can have no proof value.

Stepping-stone The first process involves the use of a 'stepping-stone' or 'intermediate impossible'. For example, if we were trying to design a safer cigarette we might say: 'Po, instead of trying to remove particles of smoke with a filter we ought to add something to them.' At first this may seem to be going in the opposite direction. Normally we might reject such a suggestion, but in lateral thinking we see where, as a stepping-stone, it can get us. What could we add? We could add air. If you make a few pinholes just above the filter of a cigarette then air is sucked in, diluting the smoke with every inhalation. Because smoke particles are deposited in the lung by Brownian motion which depends on the concentration, this dilution does in fact reduce tar deposition. I did some work on this principle many years ago. In fact the air dilution principle is now the basis of the cigarettes judged as least harmful in the USA, the United Kingdom and Germany. There are specific procedures for obtaining a stepping-stone: the easiest of these is to *reverse* whatever is happening normally. Instead of asking people to come and look at new houses, 'po, the houses go to see the people'. This stepping-stone was deliberately used by a builder in London who built a show-house on a barge in the Thames and towed it up and down the river to places to which people could easily get. Within three months he had 26,000 visitors to the house. There are also specific ways of using stepping-stones. The main principle is to use an idea deliberately as a provocation rather than reject it because it is wrong or outrageous. Where can this idea get me? The process is shown in Figure 21.

Concept-challenge This involves a deliberate focus on a concept, and a challenge *not* to its validity but to its uniqueness. Normally we challenge only those things which are inadequate or with which we can find fault. The challenge in concept-challenge is a way of saying: this is perfectly all right, but is it the *unique* and only way of looking at things? We can focus on the head of a

match and challenge why there should only be a head at one end:
this might lead to a concept of a match with two heads which
could be reversed and re-used. It is possible to challenge the round-
ness of a wheel. It is possible to challenge the uniform value of
currency: perhaps each country should have two currencies, one
of which is adjusted to keep pace with inflation by a value ex-
pressed in increasing amounts of the other (like an internal gold
standard not subject to the vagaries of international gold speculation). The concept-challenge process is more of an escape process
than a provocative one. It can, however, generate an idea which in
turn becomes a stepping-stone. The process is shown in Figure 22.
The process, and attitude, of concept-challenge is summed up in
the difference between $6+2=8$ and $8=6+2$. Both equations are
right but the first is uniquely right since carrying out the addition
operation can give no other answer. But with the second equation
'8' is not uniquely produced by adding 2 to 6 for it may be the
result of many other operations. In concept-challenge we challenge whether something is merely right (amongst alternatives) or
uniquely right.

Random juxtaposition Here the process requires the intro-
duction of a completely random stimulus which is juxtaposed with
the problem in hand. The connection that develops between the
two may serve to give emphasis to the side track, as shown in
Figure 23. For example, the juxtaposition of 'cigarette po soap'
gave rise to the idea of putting flower seeds in the butts of cigarettes so that man would beautify the surroundings with his
waste instead of messing them up. This is not a specially strong
idea, but it does illustrate the sort of idea that could not come
directly from analysis of the situation itself – although with hindsight it makes good sense. The juxtaposition of 'cigarette po
traffic-light' produced the idea of a red 'danger' band that would be
about two centimetres from the butt end of the cigarette, since the
last two centimetres are the most dangerous, as the smoke particles that have condensed there are re-evaporated. A person who
deliberately smoked into the danger zone would be making a conscious decision to do so.

There are many other techniques and processes in lateral think-

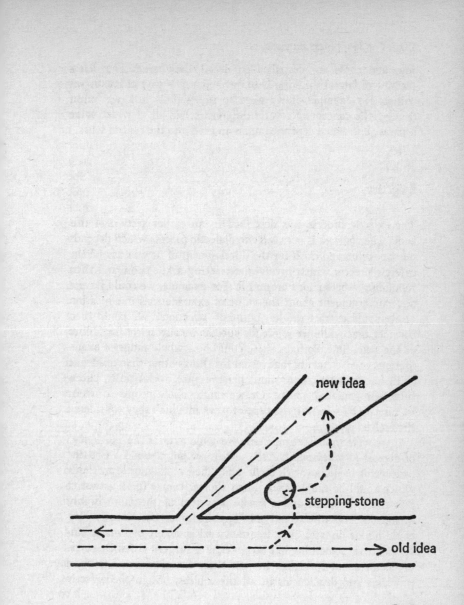

ing, and these are described in detail elsewhere.* The direct purpose of lateral thinking is to develop a new way of looking at things. For example, if we were to say 'self po leaf' we might develop the concept of several different selves all of which were separate but which depended upon and fed into the central self.

Exlectics

The exlectic process was described in an earlier section of this book. The contrast is between the dialectic process which depends on opposition and clash for the development of new ideas and the exlectic process which involves extracting a key-point and then rebuilding a better idea around it. For example, we could have a dialectic argument about the value of examinations in education or we could extract the key-point of 'selection'. We could then consider that while we select for success we also select for failure at the same time. Perhaps there could be a whole range of examinations or assessments that tested for things other than academic skill: for example, application, perseverance, social skills, cheerfulness, organizing ability. Or we might allow people to assess themselves by selecting the type of work of which they considered themselves capable.

If we were to look at medicine we could extract the 'efficiency' of doctors as a key-point. Around this we might build a two-tier concept of medicine with swift and efficient diagnostic methods which could be taught in a much shorter course (perhaps using flow-chart methods) and a back-up system of the more highly qualified doctor who would only be called upon occasionally. We could divide diseases on a frequency basis: about five major categories cover something like 80 per cent of surgery visits. One type of doctor could specialize in just these five diseases. There are problems and deficiencies in all these ideas, but in the exlectic

* *Lateral Thinking*, Penguin Books, 1971; Harper & Row, New York, 1977.

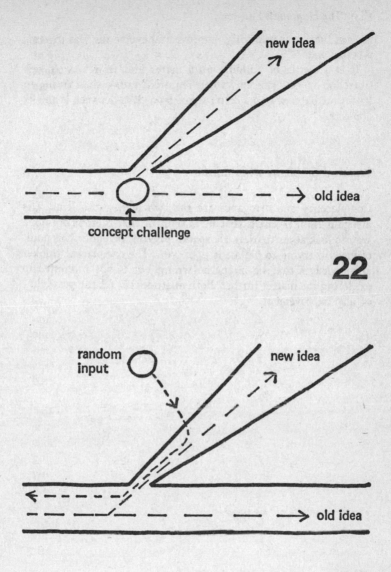

new idea

old idea

concept challenge

22

random input

new idea

old idea

23

process the aim is to modify, improve and evolve the idea towards a better one.

It is a matter of building up a better idea from the old one (introducing new concepts when required) rather than trying to batter the old idea into a better shape by a clash between it and its opposite.

Practical problems with thinking

Complacency and arrogance are the two biggest problems. The arrogant thinker insists that he is right or that there is only one way to look at a situation. He spends his time defending his point of view or trying to impose it upon you. The complacent thinker acknowledges that he might be wrong but is not interested in exploring the matter further. Both attitudes cut off the possibility of any improvement.

Unhappiness is best defined as the difference between our talents and our expectations. A two-ball juggler should not try and be a three-ball juggler unless he enjoys trying

Happiness has been defined as the coincidence of life-space and self-space, as shown in Figure 24. Since self-space is cope-space and life-space is demand-space, happiness is a cope/demand ratio of unity. That is to say, when we can cope with ease and comfort with all the pressures put upon us by the world outside and by our own selves, we can be happy. Traditional approaches to this problem have been much concerned with shrinking the life-space by detachment from this life (Buddhism); by transmitting the cares of this world into earnings for the next (Christianity) or by dropping out of the larger world into a smaller one (hippie-culture).

In order to approach the ratio of unity we can seek to reduce the life-space or to increase the self-space. Neither is very easy in practice. Nor are the two processes entirely separable – usually there is a mixture of the two. In this section we shall be looking at ways of reducing the life-space either by discarding much that is within it or by coping with some of the pressures. In the next section we shall be looking more directly at enlargement of the self-space.

Content of the life-space

The life-space is the demand-space and we can look at the different types of demand that are made upon an individual. The following list is by no means exhaustive.

Expectations The expectations set up by oneself and based on self-image and an assessment of talents that may or may not be accurate. Overall ambition with regard to role, status or position in life is usually the major expectation and demand. There may be many smaller ambitions with regard to matters of the moment: job, house, sport, marriage, etc. The expectations of others (friends, wife, family) can prove a heavy burden. If a person shows any talent at all, then the expectations are certainly bound to exceed its potential. Then there are the expectations of neighbours which have to be satisfied with regard to wealth, social status, class and the like. If a person does not keep up with these then he feels a failure and guilty, and this simply exchanges one pressure for another. Expectations may also involve the approval, attention or affection of others. Since anything that depends on others is, by definition, excluded from the self-space, these expectations – even if they are fulfilled – come into the life-space, but outside the self-space.

Pressures Fears and insecurity are the major sources of pressures. Inhibitions and timidity often make a pressure of something that could be tackled without effort. Uncertainty, misfortune and physical circumstances can all provide further pressures. Every problem that has to be solved is a pressure. Some of the problems are one-off problems which appear and then disappear when solved. Other problems, for example a personality clash with someone at work, are more long-lasting. A sick child is a pressure. Unemployment is a pressure. There are a multitude of financial and job pressures and from each of these pressures may come people pressures at work or at home.

Tensions A pressure is more easily defined than a tension. A tension is a dissatisfaction or discontentment. It is the opposite of

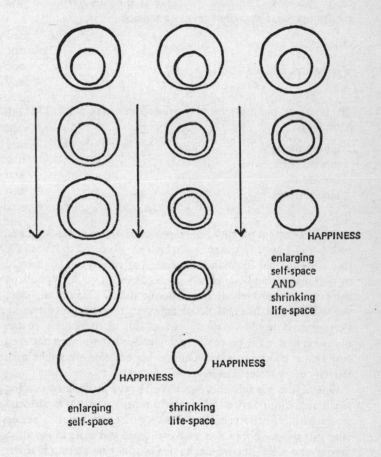

HAPPINESS

enlarging
self-space
AND
shrinking
life-space

HAPPINESS

enlarging
self-space

shrinking
life-space

24

ease. The feeling may be real enough but the cause may not be easily identifiable. A boring job of work may create tensions. Work that is too difficult and demanding may create tensions. Work that is exhausting may create tensions. Insecurity and fear may create tensions as well as pressures. Opportunities often create tensions. The need to make a difficult decision always creates tension. Depression creates a tension.

Action processes

The pressures and problems of the life-space can be reduced in four basic ways:

ignore them;
discard them;
flee them;
change them.

Ignore them

It would be nice if we could use our attention like a searchlight to pick out and amplify the things which we liked and to ignore the things we did not like. Under hypnosis attention can be directed in this manner and the effects are extraordinary. A hypnotized subject will completely ignore a needle that is piercing the skin, yet will recount in great detail an event that happened twenty years ago. It would be nice if we could, when shaving in the morning, ignore the process so completely that we were not even sure that it had taken place. On another occasion we might wish to enjoy every moment of it.

One of the big mistakes we have always made is to confuse *sensitivity* with *reaction*. We regard a sensitive person as one who reacts with sensitivity: a person who gets easily upset; a person who gets offended; a person who can sense and react to moods; a person who sulks. But we can have a sensitive mousetrap that lets down the trap with a small flop, and a sensitive mousetrap that claps the trap shut with a powerful spring. Sensitivity is on the receiving side and not necessarily on the reaction side. In theory a sensitive person could notice an insult or a slight and yet shrug and ignore it. A sensitive person could notice a slight change in the mood of another but refuse to respond to it. A sensitive person might notice a brewing crisis but refuse to react with anxiety. Because this is not usually the case, we dose people with tranquillizers in order to obtain this effect. Sensitive people often wish they were thick-skinned, but then feel that they would miss many of the more delicate joys of life.

A sensitive person is bullied by circumstances and opportunity just as a male moth is bullied by the smell of the female moth which makes him fly straight towards her from many miles away. Dogs are said to like aniseed so that a trail of aniseed will make a dog follow. In the same way a sensitive person reacts and over-reacts not only to things that are present but to things that are yet far in the future.

The solution is to develop the conscious 'shrug': that is to say, to note things but to refuse to react. It is by no means easy because instinctively we feel that sensitivity is a privilege that ought to lead to earlier action (like the deer who sniffs the approaching lion first and can flee ahead of the others).

In another section we have already seen how the 'shrug' can be used in the conflict situation in order to avoid burdening oneself with the effort of a conflict that need not arise.

There are those who seem to need the approval of others. They suffer anxieties of expectation and disappointment if it is withheld. They seem to exist only in terms of the reaction of others. But no one should feel that he has to be liked all the time. The purpose of dignity is a self-valuation that does not depend on the liking of others. As someone once told me, if she went for an audition and did not get the acting part she would console herself by saying that they were obviously looking for an apple and she was a pear. In other words, that she was not an inadequate apple but a good pear, only they wanted an apple that day. It is a useful strategy to use if someone appears to disapprove. Instead of feeling diminished by the disapproval one can always suppose that the person prefers apples – and that may be his loss.

The 'shrug' is the basis of the symbiotic give and take which makes possible situations that would otherwise be filled with problems and frictions.

To be effective the shrug must be deliberate. It is no use pretending that one has not noticed something when one has. Acknowledge the situation and consciously shrug at it.

Discard them

This is a matter of trimming the expectations and demands of the life-spaces. It is a matter of discarding ambitions which are unrealistic and cause too much trouble. It is nice to believe that one could be anything – that every private carries a field-marshal's baton in his knapsack – but in practice this is not so. Even if it were so, many people would not be willing to give up an enjoyment of life to achieve the field-marshal's position, which they rightly suspect would not be enjoyable. Most people realize that they will not be operatic singers or heavyweight boxers without too much anguish of deprivation. It is possible to apply the same realistic cut-off to other things. The criterion is whether the ambition is enjoyable *as such*. If the process of hope and work towards it is itself enjoyable then it is worth retaining. If the hope and work make for unhappiness and it is only the *arrival* at the ambition that is going to be enjoyable, then it is probably not worth keeping. Probability does come into it. Anyone who stays on longer at school is almost certain to get a more highly qualified job. But the odds in favour of making an opera singer are considerably less.

The discarding process is made more easy by recognizing differences in temperament and personality and roles. It is not much use wishing you were the extrovert of the group who was going to lead everyone else in song if you know you are not that type. Each person is a unique bag of talents and it must make more sense to find the ambition that fits those talents than the talents that fit an unthought-out ambition.

Expectations and pressures can pile up through a process of

accretion. Little things are added which at the moment of addition seem insignificant but the total is considerable. After all, the blue whale, the largest mammal in history, lives on an accumulation of sea creatures which are almost too small to see. It is easy to get into the habit of accepting tasks which other people pile on to oneself for the same reason: at the time it seems a magnanimous thing to do.

Chance is important because many things can only develop through chance. My whole involvement in the education world and the programme to teach thinking which I run at Cambridge arose because one day someone in a coffee-shop happened to pick up and read an article in a journal that was *six months* out of date. On the other hand, it is impracticable to accept everything because you can never tell what is going to come out of it. Saying 'no' is an important way to keep down the growth of the life-space – but if you say it all the time it can also keep down the growth of the self-space.

Flee them

There is nothing wrong with running away from pressures that cannot be changed but can be fled. It depends very much on the circumstances and who else is involved. There is no intrinsic virtue in facing difficulties just to have the pleasure of overcoming them. That sort of nobility is rarely rewarding enough. On the other hand it may be necessary to go through some discomfort (like learning a job) before the enjoyment begins. If one is always fleeing at the first sign of difficulty then there is going to be a perpetual flight – because fleeing gets easier each time (like divorce).

We can include the treatment of fear and anxiety under this heading because it is easier to flee the causes of fear than to overcome fear. But in this instance the flight is not a physical flight but a perceptual flight. For example, there may be a fear of something that has been experienced as frightening. Instead of conquering the fear, is it possible to look at the situation in a different way? More often there is fear of a situation *in anticipation*. The fear remains because the situation is never tried. The solution is to fly towards the situation, acknowledging that there will indeed be an initial fear but that it will pass.

A person who is worried about money may put an anti-spending clamp on his family which means that every expense becomes a worry. It is better to establish a fixed budget with freedom within it, just as it may be better to establish a diet than feel guilty about every mouthful.

Another strategy used for overcoming chronic anxiety is to spell out the worst possible thing that could happen. Once this is faced it becomes less fearful and one can even plan how to deal with it. It is unlikely that all the worst things are going to happen. And in many cases worrying about them will not prevent them happening anyway.

Anxiety-prone people are apt to try to smooth out the world in order to avoid anxiety. This is a sensible procedure but hard work. The alternative is to try to build up confidence in dealing with difficult situations: 'I don't know what is going to happen but I feel confident of my ability to cope.' That is a sort of capital investment. Circumstances can change, but what a person has invested in himself is unlikely to be lost.

Fear of making a mistake, fear of making less than a perfect deal and fear of being in the wrong are all based on an inflated ego.

If it is possible to avoid or flee the situations that cause fear, that is the best solution provided it does not mean that one stays in bed for the rest of one's life.

Change them

Bringing about a change in circumstances is a matter of problem-solving. Bringing about a new way of looking at things is a matter of perceptual change. Both should be deliberate and focused: what is the area of change, what end-product is desired?

There will be many problems that cannot be solved instantly either because they are insoluble (perhaps because they are circular: how can I get rich without making any effort?) or because a solution has not yet been found. Such problems should be defined and brought into the open rather than hidden away. An attempt can be made to turn them into 'pet-problems' which are fostered and treated with care. Or they can become 'pleasure-problems' in the sense that tackling them becomes a pleasure; they are regarded as a challenge, an opportunity rather than a pressure.

The same attempt at positive enjoyment can also be made with regard to the bother and hassle that is associated with modern life (form-filling, procedures, etc.). The timid who find it painful to face life at all can play-act a role of 'action-man' which is a sort of other-self that can be used for dealing with different situations. Most actors are very sensitive, but in playing a role their own timidity is left behind with their real selves. Just as an actor in the Japanese Noh plays holds in front of his face a mask that alters his character, so a person can develop and use masks for making situations easier. The sheep in wolf's clothing is a practicable strategy.

Tools

The specific tools with which reductions in the life-space can be brought about include:

Focus   Definition of difficult or problem areas; focus on a problem that is to be tackled; identification of source of pressure or tension; awareness of tensions and expectations. Being clear about something is the finest step towards doing something about it.

Thinking   Problem-solving; perceptual change; working things out; choices; decisions for action; assessment of priorities.

Discipline   Directed will-power. The purpose of thinking is so to arrange things that action is easy and follows the line of least effort. When this fails there may have to be an exercise of will-power to achieve an effect. This is especially so when there is a 'hump effect' that involves a period of difficulty before things get better.

Cut-off   This involves the whole area of reaction cut-off, discarding of expectations, and the 'shrug'. It is a matter of habit and training as much as anything else.

Convenience   Arranging things in the easiest manner; breaking down objectives and tasks into manageable units; making use of circumstances and opportunities; being willing to try changes that may only be temporary; making problem-solving as easy as possible; letting decisions evolve; using a creeping strategy rather than a frontal assault. Convenience is the strategy with which the other tools can be used.

Abilities and talents

It is unlikely that anyone can really change his character. But it is possible that he can improve the coping ability of his character by building on its strong points rather than trying to overcome the weaknesses. The aim in dealing with the life-space should be to increase the area which is dealt with easily rather than to set up great battlefields. Things are worth trying but rarely worth persisting in if they continue to be difficult beyond the initial stage.

As suggested earlier, it is important to recognize differences in temperament and personality and to acknowledge these. There is no such thing as a perfect all-round ideal because virtues carry disadvantages with them and vice versa. Every tree is different but nonetheless a tree.

In being realistic about oneself one can also be realistic about fluctuating moods. People do have ups and downs depending not on the poorness of their spirit but more often on the level of chemicals in their hypothalamus. It is better to recognize and sit out the poor periods by shrinking the life-space as much as possible and postponing decisions to an up period. Conversely the most should be made of up periods by making decisions, forming plans and taking action.

Sources of unhappiness

The major sources of life-space pressure can be summarized as follows:

greed: in expectations and ambitions;

anxiety: which makes a pressure of almost anything;

conflict: best treated by the 'shrug' reaction;

confusion: best treated by thinking with an emphasis on clarification and priorities;

boredom: best treated by activities and interests;

problems: best treated by problem-solving.

In all cases the fundamental questions remain: What is the pressure? Can I change it? Can I adjust to it? Am I trying to do anything about it?

Maps

As a sort of audit a life-space map can be drawn from time to time. There is no need to use geometric accuracy since the map is only symbolic. If there has been any improvement, then a dotted circle may be placed around the self-space to show an increase in this, or just inside the life-space perimeter to show a decrease in this. If a problem has been coped with then the self-space expands. If an expectation has been discarded or circumstances changed the life-space contracts.

It is well worth drawing separate life-space maps for the different selves that are involved in separate areas, such as work, hobbies, family, friends, community, outside world, etc.

Caution

It should be remembered that if life-space care becomes a *chore*, a burden, or a source of anxiety, then that is counter-effective because it is only increasing the demands.

Activity is the life-blood of the self: passivity is its bleeding

The preceding section was concerned with reducing the pressures and demands of the life-space. This could be done either by reducing the extent of the life-space (life-space shrinking) or by increasing the ability of the self to cope (self-space expansion). This section is concerned with the direct expansion of the self-space without reference to the existing pressures in the life-space.

The principle is a simple one. Self-space is defined as that part of the life-space with which the self can cope with ease (and enjoyment). So if we feed into the life-space activities which the self can cope with easily and with enjoyment then the self-space is expanded directly. It also follows that the self-space comes to take up a larger portion of the life-space even if the pressures of this have not been altered. The process is shown in Figure 25. It will be seen that addition of 'easy' activities to the life-space increases the cope/demand ratio and so brings it nearer to the unity of happiness. It also follows that in those special selves which are directly concerned with the new activities the self-space and life-space may nearly coincide in happiness.

As suggested in earlier sections, there are two distinct sorts of activity: the activity of awareness and the activity of action. The activity of awareness is an aliveness and the activity of action is a liveliness. The tennis server has the activity of action and the receiver the activity of awareness.

Activity of awareness

Although there is little or no action, the state is quite different from that of passivity. Indeed, the activity of awareness can be much more tiring than the activity of action. At least in action there is a certain momentum or continuity of action but in awareness attention can only feed on itself.

Awareness means what it suggests: intense awareness and appreciation of what is going on. The awareness may be focused or it may be general. There can be awareness of a leaf, of a bird's song, of a pop record, of the taste of a hamburger, of the traffic noise in a city street, of a poem, of the way a person walks or smiles, of silence, of shaving, or of anything. The awareness is an awareness of appreciation – an appreciation of something for being in existence and for being what it is. In Eastern cultures this is often termed the 'isness' of something.

In addition to the sheer appreciation of 'isness' there can be an appreciation of a more cultured sort of beauty – for example, the beauty of a fragrance in a garden or of a rose. This may be a matter of sensitization and interest. A person who knows a lot about a particular painter may become aware of the subtle change in his style in a particular painting. Clearly this extra awareness does require some background knowledge or sensitization.

In the activity of action there is a large mixture of awareness and appreciation of what is happening as the activity is being carried through.

The moment

Usually we fail to appreciate the moment because we are looking beyond it to what comes next. We travel down a road to get somewhere. We shave in the morning to have shaved. We greet someone so that an absence of greeting will not be thought ill-mannered. We look at a glass and wish it were full of something to drink rather than appreciating it as an object in its own right. We tend to be too interested in use and what comes next and how things fit together. This follows directly from the patterns of our perception which link things together. We hurry along the track of a pattern and no longer notice the individual items. The process is shown in Figure 26 which suggests that we ought to stop in this headlong rush and concentrate with intensity on the moment.

Just as awareness is rewarding so is it difficult. That is why it is regarded as an activity. It requires practice and training. Now and then one should pause and really savour the moment. One should also practice concentrating for brief spells on things that happen to be around: the pen on the desk, the sound of the doorbell, a patch of grass. The third type of training involves practising an awareness of the general mood of the moment whether it includes oneself or not: the mood in the street or in a restaurant; the mood of another person. This awareness is often referred to as a sort of 'third' eye which watches in order to savour whereas the other two eyes watch in order to use and to move on. One can savour a word, a phrase, an idea or the space between ideas.

Activity of action

Tibetans say their prayers by turning a prayer wheel. The Hindu's life is full of definite rituals which are supposed to be performed several times a day. The Moslem gets down on his prayer mat at the appointed times. The Catholic goes to mass on Sundays. All these rituals can be done mechanically. It is probably intended that they should keep the believer in touch with his belief and with God. It is also intended that the praying soul should take part in the rituals, which should not be mechanical. But purely as mechanical functions they have an immense value. There can be the same sort of value as there is with the intricate Judaic law (concerning food and other matters) which orthodox Jews follow. This is the value of involvement. But there is also the sheer value

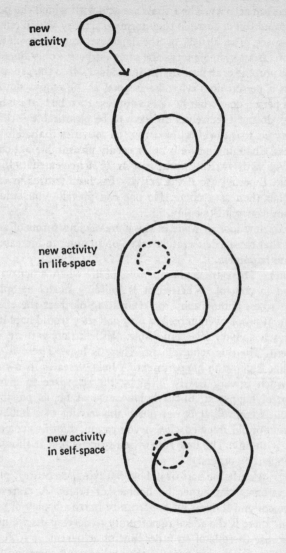

new
activity

new activity
in life-space

new activity
in self-space

25

of mechanical activity. The rituals are acts with which the person *can cope and feel at ease*. So they form an activity which enlarges his self-space. The rituals of the Japanese work song and the rituals of Fascist systems serve the same purpose – only here they serve the purpose of abdicating the individual self to the group self.

When a person does what he is good at, he enjoys doing it. When a person does what he does with ease then he is at ease. The activities do not themselves all have to be pleasurable – though they may be. It is the effect of doing the activities that adds up to happiness. Changing a tyre is not specially pleasurable but changing a tyre with swiftness and ease is an achievement which is enjoyable. Especially so if the activity has been treated as enjoyable rather than as a chore. No one can prevent you enjoying something you want to enjoy.

We can now look at some of the more obvious forms of action activity that can be deliberately taken up in order to increase self-space and happiness.

Hobbies   These are deliberate areas of life where a person is at ease and in control. Whether it is building model aeroplanes, growing roses, photography, or renovating old cars the effect is the same. If people were forced to play golf they would hate it, but as a chosen activity it is enjoyable. With a hobby there is involvement. There is achievement. There is hope. There is something that is going to happen next. A hobby creates its own life-space which is very nearly filled by the self-space to give the equation of happiness. But a hobby must as far as possible be under one's control. It is not much use having as a hobby the renovation of old stage coaches if you cannot afford to come into contact with any. The first rule of self-space is that it should not be dependent on others.

Craft   A craft is a sort of hobby. Weaving, carpentry, plumbing, electronics can either be hobbies or crafts. A craft offers achievement and it offers an opportunity for the display of talent. In a craft there is the added opportunity to develop discipline and will, because there is often a deadline of achievement to be met. Few writers would ever write if they relied on inspiration. They have to develop a discipline which makes them sit down at a

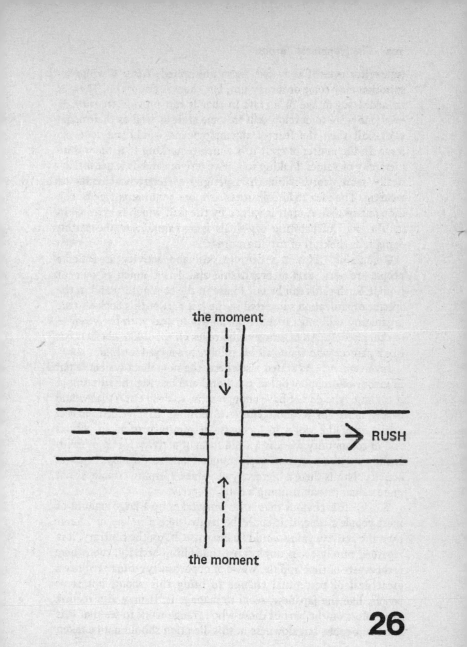

the moment

RUSH

the moment

typewriter even if they feel most uninspired. After a while inspiration may come or it may not, but the writer goes on. There is an added advantage in a craft in that it can provide security. If everyone were to develop skill in some craft as well as their usual work-skill then the fear of unemployment would not loom so large. In the matter of craft it is worth remarking that there is *no* hierarchy of values. Making folk jewellery or sandals is not intrinsically more worth-while than designing electronic circuits or welding. The idea that 'folksiness' is more genuine is part of the drop-out system. A craft is valued by the skill which is invested in it. The craft of painting egg-shells is as valuable to the person doing it as the craft of carving statues.

Organizing This is a definite skill and activity area. Some people are very good at organizing and derive much enjoyment from it. Such skills can be put to use in the community and in the specific organization suggested in the last part of this book. A true organizing skill must include the ability to deal with the vagaries of other people. An organizer who relies on robot-like obedience is like a painter who wants all his colours pre-mixed for him.

Involvement As stated elsewhere, the new meta-system is not in favour of dropping out of the world and leaving the running of it to those who do not have enough sense to drop out – that would hardly make for its most effective running. Involvement in the activities of the world in business, in administration, in politics and in community work is a valid form of activity for enjoyment. It may require a certain temperament, but so do most types of activity. Nor is there a hierarchy of values. Helping cripples is not more valuable than running a bank properly.

Work It is obvious that since work takes up a large amount of most people's time, if it could be treated like a hobby or a craft then the activity value would be immense. If, on the contrary, it is regarded purely as an unpleasant time-filling activity, then there is the waste of time and the waste of opportunity. It may require a great deal of perceptual change to bring this about, but some people, like the Japanese, seem to manage it. It may also require some effort on the part of those who arrange work to see that it is more enjoyable, but slowness in this direction should not be taken as an excuse for not trying to make work personally enjoyable. Some constructivity here is more valuable than negativity.

Helping others This form of activity has always been the stand-by of most religious meta-systems because it has a social value and a value in overcoming selfishness. It remains a very satisfying form of activity and one for which there are always opportunities. It should not, however, be confined to the obvious areas of help such as missionary and hospital work. In everyday life there is ample opportunity for the exercise of 'positive respect' which means a deliberate effort to enlarge the self-space of another by helping him cope with his problem.

Interest Specializing in a particular field is another area of activity. There are so many different fields today that it is not difficult to become an expert in one of them. A friend of mine became an expert in Chinese armorial porcelain because he inherited a few pieces. You could become an expert in left-handed snails if you wished. The important point is that the achievement should lie in the interest itself – not because you want to be the world's expert and will be unhappy until you are recognized as such. Learning new subjects at college or university is another activity area. So is collecting things and games-playing.

Sport This is a traditional area of activity, but it is probably less useful than others because nowadays the emphasis is so heavily on professionalism and competition that the enjoyment has been reduced. The more healthy type of competition is the 'band-width' type as in Judo. Here a person can progress through different coloured belts and thus feel he is improving. Success is not just a matter of beating someone else and coming first. There is another danger with sport and that is that it can become a passive time-filling exercise – something that is done in order to avoid having to find something else to do.

Television This is probably the best example of time-filling passive activity. In their pictures children tend to include TV sets as 'furniture' in rooms but not as a part of 'fun-machines'. Television could be a source of awareness activity like the theatre or the cinema, but it is so very easy to *start* watching television as the minimal activity which will pre-empt the need to find something to do, and then to go on watching. It is useful to get into the habit of having a deliberate 'television gap' of an hour every evening during which the set is switched off. As such, television does very little for the self except overload it with information.

Achievement

Achievement and awareness are part of the enjoyment of activity. Achievement needs to be the achievement of performance rather than that of destination. As with looking, the habit of keeping one's eyes only on the future prevents enjoyment of the now. In activity now-care is more important than future-care (it is in *thinking* that there has to be a balance).

The dependence on others for approval makes any activity less satisfying and can create pressures. The singer who has to find an audience, the concert pianist who has to be offered a concert are obvious examples. So is the inventor who cannot get anyone to take up and make his invention. These are situations of frustration which serve to load the life-space with self-generated expectations and so serve to diminish the self-space. The approval of others is a bonus but should not be the essence of achievement.

Intensity

If nothing is really worth doing, then everything is worth doing properly. This is so because the purpose of the activity now becomes the enjoyment of the self and that depends on the same sort of intensity that is required for awareness activity. It is an attitude covered by the Latin motto *age quod agis*, or 'do what you do'. It is a fullness of doing that can turn a task from a boring chore to something enjoyable. It is an investment of effort that returns rewards of enjoyment. It is the opposite of sloppiness and time-filling. Sloppiness saves very little effort but completely destroys the possibility of the task being enjoyable or a source of achievement. Sloppiness is counter-effective as regards the self. Sloppiness is passively being carried along by the job instead of doing it. Sloppiness drains the self rather than fuels it.

Plurality

Different people have different talents. Find what you can do most easily and make it important for you to do it. Effort and discipline may be required but they yield much better dividends when they are applied in an area that is in tune with a person's talents than when they have to be used instead of talents. From time to time everyone should self-indulge in an EPA exercise. This stands for an Exercise in Positive Assessment. It is not meant to be an honest assessment of a total person, but just a search for the positive attributes: the talents and the things which are easy and enjoyable to do. Activity can then be built around these.

Stone-cutters' religion

Activity is so important that one could almost invent a religion in which the *sole* requirement was that every person would be involved in carving a stone image of a particular idol. When they came to the end of one image they would start on another. And they would never ask the reason why.

In happiness as in cooking there is a brew of ingredients to suit different tastes

Every individual can construct his own happiness profile based on what he knows of his own personality and the opportunities open to him. Does he want a steady profile, perhaps even a climbing one? Or does he want a profile characterized by peaks with the inevitable troughs in between? Some examples of profiles are shown in Figure 27.

The ingredients of happiness have been listed before in their more recognizable forms. The happiness profile can include as much or as little as a person wishes of peace, joy, interest, enthusiasm, pleasure and excitement. It is somewhat like cooking and deciding on the right balance of ingredients to suit a particular taste. The taste may vary with experience and as one gets older.

In setting up a happiness profile it is useful to keep certain things in mind.

Distraction Something which is not really enjoyable in itself but only in so far as it precludes doing something else.

Counter-effective When something which is intended to produce happiness ends up by having the opposite effect. For example, over-indulgence in the pleasure of eating creates indigestion, and pure dependence on excitement creates boredom.

Effort-expensive When the amount of effort (in work, waiting and cost) is out of proportion to the rewards. There may be much better investments of effort that can be made.

Continuity Carrying on with something not because it is

EXCITEMENT

EQUILIBRIUM

MOOD

EQUILIBRIUM

PEACE

EQUILIBRIUM

enjoyable any longer but because stopping requires a decision for which there seem to be no grounds.

Green-field effect The idea that something unknown must necessarily be more enjoyable than what is known.

Sensitization The process of increasing sensitivity so that the same thing becomes more and more enjoyable. It is the opposite of habituation in which something which was once enjoyable has become stale.

Trade-off The need to appreciate that it may not be possible to have everything at once. Something may have to be given up deliberately in order to enjoy something else.

Cut-off The point at which further effort in the same direction is unlikely to be worth-while. An appreciation of balance.

Happiness audit

A happiness profile is for the future. It is your guess of what suits your temperament. You are quite likely to be wrong but you can only find this out if you have a means with which to compare what happens with what you thought would happen. With a happiness profile you can look back and see if the opportunities were there and, if they were, whether the profile did really suit your temperament. A happiness audit is the same thing applied to the past. You look back and see over the preceding years what sort of things have happened and how you have been seeking your happiness. Is there much of it and if so how and where did it come about?

Happiness foundation

The basic foundation for happiness in the new meta-system is the coincidence of the self-space and the life-space as discussed in the preceding sections. This, in association with dignity (coincidence of self-space and ego), gives a person who is at ease with himself and with the world and can therefore enjoy both of them. It gives a system that is fully functioning. The addition of pleasure, joy, peace, excitement and the other ingredients is either on top of this foundation or a means of enlarging the self-space. They are subservient to the basic process of enlarging self-space or coping with the life-space.

If more is better, how can yet more be worse?

We have never really solved the problem of balance. If we could solve the problem of balance we could solve the problem of human behaviour. That is why throughout the ages philosophers and preachers have exhorted their listeners to observe the Golden Mean, to practise moderation and to imitate the harmony of nature. Aesthetics is almost pure balance.

The reason balance is so extremely difficult is that it goes against the two basic human systems of appetite and perception. As far as appetite goes, if something is attractive, it is attractive. It is not possible for something to be attractive and unattractive at the same time without driving the animal neurotic. So the thing is attractive. *After* the thing has been enjoyed then a cut-off mechanism comes into play which indicates that a sufficiency has been taken. These cut-off mechanisms are based in the hypothalamus and do sometimes go wrong, giving rise to such disorders as under-eating and over-eating. But the main point is that the cut-off is never part of the perception of the attraction. That remains *pure* attraction. So in areas where there is no natural cut-off the human mind has to supply one by exercising balance.

The second reason why balance is so difficult is that perception only deals in fixed patterns. We can distinguish one colour from another because they are different and have different names. But if we are dealing with a spectrum of grey from white to black then it is much more difficult to recognize and deal with the greys except through comparison. We know that lack of sun is unpleasant, so it follows that sunshine is a good thing. But we also know that too much sunshine is also unpleasant. So how much is enough? We can define it in a circular fashion by saying that enough is enough for it to be pleasant, but this is useless. We can put a value to the hours of sunshine or the degree of temperature and then we can deal with the spectrum from none to too much in a more definite way. But in many areas we are not able to put a scale on the spectrum. If you are dealing with a situation, how much force is enough?

Types of balance

There are in fact three distinct types of balance: the spectrum type, the mix type and the alternation type. Each of these will be considered separately.

The spectrum type of balance Here it is a matter of establishing the balance point along a spectrum that ranges from one extreme to another. We know that if traffic does not move at all there will be no accidents. We may know that if traffic moves as fast as it likes there will be many accidents. Where do we establish the balance point for the speed limit so that we do have movement but not too many accidents? We have seen the spectrum type of balance as applied to the desirability of sunshine. It could also be applied to the problem of centralization and de-centralization. How much should a government do centrally and how much should local authorities do themselves? A purer example of the spectrum type of balance is that of self-love. At one extreme there is egotism and arrogance and at the other extreme there is disgust with the self. Somewhere along the spectrum is the point at which self-love is dignity. In fact dignity has been defined in exact terms elsewhere in this book. There is a spectrum from social drinking of alcohol to alcoholism; where is the danger point?

The mix type of balance Here it is a matter of mixing together the right balance of ingredients, as in making a sauce or cocktail. For example, there might have to be the right balance between freedom and structure, between leadership and initiative, between free enterprise and a planned economy, between direct and indirect taxes, between performance and looks in the purchase of a car.

The alternation type of balance In some ways this is just a special case of the mix type except that the mix is in *time*. It is the proportion of time allotted to each ingredient that gives the balance. But each ingredient operates fully for that amount of time. For example, a school may have a balance between sport and academic work – but each fully occupies the time allotted to it. The alternation between lateral and logical thinking is one such balance. So is the alternation between now-care and future-care and the alternation between attention to the inner world and to the outer world.

Dealing with balance

Being able to cope with balance is as fundamental to the new meta-system as it is to many other meta-systems. Some of the general precepts indicated below may be applied for this purpose.

Recognition and audit A sort of stocktaking can be of great help. A person looks into his own life and sees how much balance there is with regard to two opposing possibilities (for example the balance between now-care and future-care). Simply by looking at the situation he may find that there is not nearly as much balance as he might wish. There can then be a deliberate attempt to even up the balance or at least make it match some plan. It is rarely a matter of a fifty-fifty balance, but if an audit reveals that something is being done exclusively then obviously there is a case for giving some attention to the other aspect.

Middle-place concepts In the spectrum type of balance problem it may be useful to *create* a middle-place concept. Thus, in the alcohol example one might create three concepts: social drinking, heavy drinking and alcoholism. This makes it easier to place one-self in one of the categories or at least to know which category to aim for. Or, in the egotism example we could have the three cat-egories: self-effacement, confidence, arrogance. We can now aim for the middle one instead of trying to keep a balance between the two extremes. This is not unlike the red-amber-green sequence of some traffic lights.

Personality Some people will always choose the same recog-nizable items on a menu whereas others will always try some-thing new. Some people will always want to return to a place where they had enjoyed a holiday whereas others will prefer to experiment with somewhere new. There is an individual prefer-ence for change and adjustment and for inward-directed activity and outward-directed activity. It is useful to be aware of one's own personality type. The next stage would be to resist a tendency to carry the preference to extremes. For example, if you never tried anywhere new or any new dish you might be missing an oppor-tunity that would have been enjoyed.

Counter-effective This concept can be developed and used. For example, pleasure is pleasurable up to a point, but beyond that point it can become counter-effective. Once the concept is estab-lished it is possible to ask oneself whether a situation has passed the balance point and so become counter-effective. In the same bracket we can put the concepts of addiction and dependence. Is there an addiction to excitement? Is there a dependence on novelty? Looking at matters in terms of such concepts makes it easier to operate a balance. 'Effort-expensive' is another such con-cept. Something may still be attractive and worth doing, but is it really worth all the effort which might be better used elsewhere? Has something become too effort-expensive beyond the balance-point?

Trade-off This is a very useful concept derived from the business world. It means that something may have to be given up in order to achieve something else. The main point is that the thing that is being given up is still *attractive*. There is no attempt to deny its attractiveness, for it is such denial which leads to the failure of so many balance procedures. For someone who is dieting it is absurd to pretend that further food will not taste nice, but it may make sense to offer a trade-off between further food and personal attractiveness. Similarly there can be a trade-off between excitement and peace. Some excitement has to be deliberately given up if peace is to be enjoyed. The secret of a successful trade-off is to make the *giving up* decision the deliberate one. It is not a matter of what you choose, but of what you choose to give up.

Cut-off This is another useful concept also derived from the business world, and it suggests that there comes a point at which something is no longer worth doing and so a cut-off is exercised. For example, there can be a cut-off in an effort to change circumstances, and a switch is now made towards adjustment to them.

Sequence In some cases it is possible to set up a sequence for each side of the balance. For example, you might try to alter circumstances first and then adjust to them if you cannot. You could also try to give freedom to a classroom first and then if this did not work introduce some structure.

Artificial proportions It may help in some cases to establish artificial proportions with regard to a mix or alternation type of balance. For example, you may decide to spend 5 per cent of the time on lateral thinking and the rest on logical thinking, when faced with a problem. Or you may decide to spend one third of your time on awareness-type activity and two thirds on action-type activity. The figures will always be arbitrary and it is very unlikely that you could ever stick to them, but it can help as a sort of guideline.

Balance areas

We can now consider some of the balance areas that have arisen at one time or another in this book.

Adjustment and change The fundamental balance problem as to whether one should adjust to circumstances or try to change them. It largely depends on the personality and the ease of changing the circumstances. If possible, it is easier to change them than to make the perceptual change required for adjustment. It also depends on whether a person enjoys trying to make the change or only the result of it.

Involvement and drop-out To shrink the life-space is encouraged, but a total drop-out is not. A drop-out for a period of time may, however, be useful. This is a spectrum-type problem: how far to get involved. Personality also comes into it a great deal.

Now-care and future-care Enjoyment should be directed at now-care, but thinking must take some account of future-care. Usually this is a matter of redressing an almost exclusive emphasis on future-care at the expense of now-care.

Ignore and react How far should one ignore an event (shrug) and how far should one react? If one is inclined to over-react then deliberately put the emphasis on the ignore side. It is the actual importance of the event that matters – not one's feelings in the matter.

Inner world and outer world Should one spend most time on contemplation and consideration of the inner world or on consideration of the outer world? This would seem to be an area for a deliberate setting of a proportion. The tendency is for one type of personality to concentrate exclusively on the inner world and another exclusively on the outer.

Awareness activity and action activity This will depend very much on circumstances. For instance, an old person may have less opportunity for action activity. People who are heavily engaged in action activity should, however, make a definite effort to spend some time in awareness activity, as this can easily be neglected.

Projective and reactive action Does one just react to circumstances or does one occasionally initiate the action? It is a matter for personal audit. On the whole, most people spend *all* the time reacting and therefore some effort should be made to initiate action – even when one seems fully occupied with reactions to events.

Excitement and peace Depends on circumstances and even more on personality. Peace is more dependable and excitement more effort-expensive. It depends also on what level of excitement is required. A trade-off is probably required here, and also the happiness profile exercise suggested in another section.

Stability and change   Does one seek to keep something exactly as it is or to change it? This depends on the nature of the thing. Obviously an ancient ceremony should be kept as it is but an inefficient way of serving meals in a canteen should be changed. It depends on the room for change and the advantages that are expected to follow the change. It is best not to take a conservative or revolutionary stance in advance and as a *habit*.

Prejudice and doubt   Should one act on the certainty of prejudice or wait in doubt for fuller information? This depends on the purpose and urgency of the thinking. In practice the best educated guess which is somewhere between the two extremes is preferable. This is another spectrum problem.

Lateral and logical thinking   Changing concepts only takes a short time but developing and using the new concept may be a much longer process. So more time will be spent on logical thinking, and lateral thinking will be used to generate new directions. After all, if you change direction at each step you will not get far. What is important is that lateral thinking should be used deliberately: too often it is supposed that logical analysis *alone* is sufficient.

Self and society   How much time and attention should be spent on one and how much on the other? This is a matter of mix and alternation and circumstances. What is important is that some time should be spent on each.

Structure and freedom   This is usually a heavily polarized position. On the one side there are those who believe that any mention of structure destroys all freedom and spontaneity. On the other side are those who feel that freedom is chaos and mess. Both sides are wrong. There is a need for a liberating structure which, acting as a framework, actually increases the range of freedom and certainly its effectiveness. This is a mix type of problem in practice. It is a matter of setting up structure envelopes within which a person can be free.

Perfect balance

No one is ever going to achieve a perfect balance in any situation. The best that can be hoped for is to avoid an exclusive emphasis on one or other side of the balance. There is a balancing skill in driving a car along the road: preventing it from going into the ditch and from hitting the oncoming traffic. We need to give as much attention to the balancing skills in our lives and take as much pride in their performance.

The paradox is that the great emphasis on self in the new meta-system prevents selfishness because other selves are regarded as equally important – that is the process of respect

It must seem that a meta-system that puts the highest emphasis on self – as does the new meta-system – would run into trouble with relationships. The traditional meta-systems have tried to subjugate self because self leads to selfishness and this upsets the relationship of man to his fellows and to society as well as to his salvation. To claim that self is all right up to a point and that then it becomes selfishness is impractical and weak and just a way of evading the issue.

A meta-system which encouraged selfishness would suggest a *laissez-faire* system in which the strong triumphed and the weak were subjugated. Paradoxically it is precisely because the new meta-system is so strongly in favour of self that the *laissez-faire* system is inappropriate.

The solution to the dilemma is quite straightforward. The emphasis on self applies not only to an individual's own self but to *all the different selves around him*. The emphasis on self protects his self but also protects the others. The other selves include other people but also the 'self' of the community and the social system.

If for self we read 'system' then the new meta-system is in favour of the *full functioning* of a system without interference from other systems. The human systems are to function in parallel within the framework of the community and social system.

The difference between the three states of denial of self,

denial of self

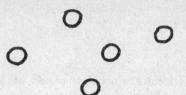

selfishness

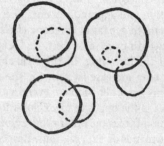

free for all

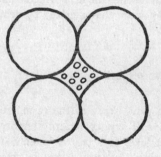

new meta-system

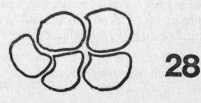

28

selfishness and *laissez-faire* (free for all) and the new meta-system is suggested in Figure 28.

Respect

The fundamental principle of respect has been mentioned in earlier sections. It is the 'space' between selves that allows each one to function as a separate unit with its own worth. In order to understand the concept of respect it is useful to look at the concepts of exploitation and aggrandisement. These can be summed up in the expression: 'to get fat at someone else's expense'. Aggrandisement is the fattening up of a self, and exploitation of others is the source of the fattening. In the terms of the new meta-system this is not a true increase in self, for the self-space must contain no dependence on other people – even in an exploiting sense.

Respect is the opposite of exploitation and aggrandisement. Respect is non-intrusion upon other selves. This intrusion can be by way of demands or expectations. Respect allows for a mutual 'contractual' arrangement in which there is a symbiotic give and take but this is not characterized by demands and expectations.

Positive respect

In the usual sense of the term, 'respect' tends to be neutral or negative. It implies non-interference. But in the new meta-system respect takes on a *positive* aspect. You do not respect a grave by neglecting to go near it but by seeing that it is cared for and by placing flowers on it occasionally. You do not respect a person by turning your back on him or ignoring him but by a positive greeting. Respect therefore includes the two principles:

avoiding intrusion upon the self of another;
an effort to increase that self.

The ultimate effect is not unlike the aristocratic tradition of *noblesse oblige*. A person who is at ease with his own self does not seek to support it at the expense of others and has time to try to increase the selves of others. The power of positive respect is the sort of power encouraged in the new meta-system.

The three respects

The three respects that have been mentioned earlier are: respect for oneself; respect for other individuals; respect for the social system. The social system covers the community, the state and the world at large. It is on these three respects that a value and ethical system can be built. At the bottom the fundamental consideration is that of 'system ethics'; the proper functioning of a system according to its nature.

In earlier sections we have considered man's respect for his own self and the concept of dignity (coincidence of ego and self-space). In this section we shall deal specifically with man's relationship to other men and to the social system in which he lives.

Relationship between individuals

What is written here is intended as the minimal foundation upon which more intense and more loving relationships can be built. But it is suggested that such relationships should at least have respect as a foundation. Love cannot really be a substitute for respect – even though it may seem so for a short while.

Non-intrusion

The principle governing relationships between individuals is that of non-intrusion and positive respect. Intrusion can take many forms. There are demands which one individual makes upon another. There are expectations whereby one individual saddles another with an expectation. It may be a matter of setting an expectation for another person or expecting that person to do something for you. Many people expect others to run or smooth their lives for them. Many people demand help, consideration or sympathy as a right. Many people fling out responsibilities like grappling hooks.

Envy is an intrusion upon another. So is manipulation. Games-playing and deception are further intrusions. It is obvious that the 'use' of other people constitutes that exploitation which is the opposite of respect.

There are, however, give-and-take situations in which the two parties are in a state of symbiosis. This is a sort of contractual relationship in which the areas of give and take are mutually defined. For example, the relationship between two individuals may involve a dominant and following role. These roles usually oscillate with one party being dominant at one time and then the other taking over. It is not unlike two children on opposite ends of a see-saw. One is prepared to jump up in the air so that the other can come down and then the roles reverse.

The loading of demands, pressures and expectations upon another increases his life-space and thereby, relatively, decreases his self-space. If, however, in the process of positive respect a person welcomes this extra load because he can cope with it, then he is increasing his own self-space. Positive respect means increasing the self-space of another by helping him cope with his own life-space. But this must be voluntary. It cannot be a matter of forcing your load of troubles on to someone else. As a form of activity, taking over someone else's troubles can be an effective way of increasing self-space – for those who can cope with it.

Relationship between individual and society

It is in the interest of most individuals that there should be some sort of social system. This is the opposite of an anarchy which benefits very few and eventually not even those few. Thus respect for the social system or the state is really a form of respect for others and for oneself – not because the state is representative but because some form of social order is beneficial.

Respect for the social system involves respect for the law. Those who consider themselves above the law are the system-cheats who operate the ethic of 'what you can get away with'. Their punishment should fit not the crime but the *effort* society has to make to keep itself protected from them.

Does this mean that any social or political system is worthy of respect? The answer is that in so far as it provides a framework for living it is worthy of respect, but that does not mean that attempts cannot be made to alter it. The valuation of a social or political system would depend on whether or not it exhibited the three respects: respect for individuals, respect for other social systems, respect for the larger system of the world as a whole. Attempts to alter or improve the system can come under three headings: regulation, modification and replacement.

Regulation There may be areas where the behaviour of a political system may need restraining. Action in this regard is part of the process of the system itself. There are other times when action in some area may have to be initiated by the public through protests or demonstrations. Again this is part of the regulatory process.

Modification This includes matters like the change of government in a democratic system. Almost by definition, adherents of the new meta-system would tend to be floating voters because their votes would be determined by their respect for the social system as such rather than a particular party doctrine. At different times one or other party would seem to provide the best answers. Excessive party loyalty is the sort of abdication of self and thinking that runs counter to the principles of the metasystem.

Replacement The replacement of a total political system is a matter of difficulty. Clearly there are systems which may need replacing. On the other hand, opposition for the sake of opposition can be decided by reference to the answers to three basic questions:

1 Is the opposition designed to be negative or constructive? In other words, is a positive alternative offered?
2 At whose expense is the improvement going to be made? There must be a clear and realistic appraisal of this: such vague notions as taxing the rich or big business are myths, not reality.
3 For whose immediate benefit is the exercise of opposition mounted? The consideration is whether the exercise is for the emotional aggrandisement of individuals or a group or really for the benefit of everyone.

Positive respect and the social system

The principle of positive respect applies even more strongly here than in the matter of relationships between individuals. There are some who operate on the 'gimme' principle in the belief that if the state exists it has a duty to provide for the wants of anyone who happens to exist. This shows a rather one-sided view of the principle of positive respect. Neutral respect would demand that the state did not interfere with the lives of individuals. Positive respect would demand that the state went further and helped the lives of individuals – but in return the individual would be expected to show positive respect towards the state and not feel that his mere existence was enough contribution. In the words of John Kennedy, 'ask not what your country can do for you but what you can do for your country'. The same principle applies to the smaller social system of the community or family.

As part of its 'self' and its coping, the state has an obligation to care for the sick and unfortunate, but it does not have an obligation to help those who are unwilling to help themselves. This is because it is assumed that everyone is willing to include in his life-space some demand for help for the unfortunate, but the same cannot be assumed for the lazy.

Priorities

The principle of respect suggests that all the different selves can live in harmony. There are times, however, when a decision needs to be made in favour of one self or another. We can look at the priorities in three areas: attention, conflict and action.

Attention   The priorities in terms of attention would be: (1) self; (2) community; (3) outside world. This is because the happiness and strength of the self lead to a happy community which in turn leads to a happier world.

Conflict   If there is a conflict of interests where a proposed action could harm one area while benefiting another, the priorities would be: (1) outside world; (2) community; (3) self. This is not a matter of selflessness but of practical self-interest. The self is embedded in the community which in turn is embedded in the world. For example, to pollute the world for the benefit of a community would be short-sighted.

Action   In matters of positive action the priorities would again be different: (1) community; (2) self; (3) outside world. This is because action as such will benefit the self and therefore there is more sense in action which, while benefiting the self, also benefits the community. Action in the outside world is of course important, but it can be community action.

Dialectic

In all matters of relationships the wasteful dialectics of 'we' and 'they' are to be avoided. This is because in the dialectic framework action that is fundamentally negative can *seem* to be positive and constructive. Opposition for the sake of opposition can *seem* to be for the benefit of all. If we discard the dialectic model, then constructive action really has to be constructive.

Failure of respect

We can recognize deficiencies or failures of respect with regard to the respect which a person has for himself and also the respect he ought to hold for others and for the structure of society. Failures of self-respect include self-abdication, dropping-out, passivity, self-pity, negativism, egotism (as the opposite of dignity), complacency, irresponsibility and over-reaction (the creation of self-pressures). Failures of respect with regard to others include arrogance, system-cheats, bullying, intolerance, excessive dependence (an abdication of responsibility), unique-truthers (imposing unique truths on others), negativism and destructiveness, and takers (relying on cunning, manipulation and charm). Most of these processes have been discussed in an earlier section of the book.

It must be admitted that the new meta-system has nothing as strong as hell-fire to keep people in order. There is a concept of failure rather than sin. The best sanction against failure of respect is awareness. This is both awareness within a person as he observes his own behaviour and a social awareness as society observes the misbehaviour of those who show no respect for others. Awareness does not have to be descriptive, passive or resigned – it can be translated into more definite action. The first step is for an individual, or society, to define the behaviour that shows an unacceptable lack of respect. Such behaviour need not be dependent on basic morals or ethics but on the needs of society as a functioning system that requires respect if it is to function smoothly.

Part Three
Action

The structure of the new meta-system is the soil from which grow the principles that, like vegetables, can be used

In this section we can summarize in a definite manner the action steps that are involved in the new meta-system. The ten steps listed below are only a beginning but they cover the main points.

1 Mood and attitude

Positive and constructive This includes hope; looking on the bright side; building things up rather than knocking them down; and building on the positive aspects of man's nature.

Anti-negative Avoidance of negativity; complaining; perpetual opposition; and deriving a joy from attacking.

Happiness and enjoyment Recognizing the deliberate pursuit of happiness as a legitimate purpose of life; a willingness to enjoy life and to set up things to be enjoyed; an attempt to change problems and pressures into a source of enjoyment.

Self Recognizing the huge importance of self and especially of dignity; recognizing that other selves are important as well.

Respect The three basic respects for self, others and the social system. This also includes the importance of positive respect which goes beyond non-interference.

Anti-passivity Avoidance of passivity; drift; time-filling; and the abdication of self.

This can all be summed up as a positive attitude and an emphasis on self and happiness.

2 Review and audit

This is an important part of the new meta-system because of the emphasis on self and the need to avoid drift. Review and audit are concerned with an honest look at oneself. This is not an examination of conscience in the sense of seeking out faults for self-recrimination. It is rather a search for opportunities to increase happiness. An audit of the status quo gives one something to react to. An audit provides a *map* on which action can be based. The process of audit and review also includes recognition – for example, the recognition of one's own moods or over-reactivity. This audit and review is intended as an individual exercise which each person carries out for himself from time to time. It can include the following.

Life-space maps   Drawing life-space maps showing the relation of self-space to life-space. This can be an overall life-space map, but there should also be separate maps for the different areas of self; personal, family, work, hobbies, community, etc. This family of maps can give a better general picture.

Happiness-profile and audit   A definition and recognition of personality and circumstances in an effort to assess the personal make-up of happiness. This can refer to the past in terms of the audit or to the future in the profile. The procedure is a very general one. For example, one person may derive most happiness from his work whereas another may derive it from his friends. Excitement may be important to some people whereas peace is important to others.

EPA   An exercise in positive assessment. This involves having a look at the strong points in one's personality and situation and making a note of the things that are done with ease and enjoyment. The process is an attempt to show up the areas that can be most easily built upon. It can also emphasize the individuality of a person (as opposed to the idea that there is one sort of 'perfect person').

Recognize Recognize the ups and downs of moods which may well have a physical basis in the hypothalamus. Once the moods are recognized they can be adjusted to.

Identify There may be whole areas of passivity, drift and time-filling which need to be recognized. It is not a matter of feeling guilty about them or even trying to eradicate them all at once. It is merely a review of the situation – with the possibility of future action.

3 Focus and objectives

Focusing upon something and then dealing with it is more difficult than it seems. The major fault is lack of focus or focus on too large a problem. For example, a person may focus on the need to change his whole job instead of on what is wrong with it or how it can be made more enjoyable. The purpose of focus is to set up definite areas of attention or tasks that can be done. The emphasis should always be on a sharp focus on a small area. The focus can always be enlarged later. There is a place for general mood and feeling, but the process of specific and definite focus is essential.

Problems Focusing on specific problems and on the sub-problem that may lie beneath. Problem-'finding' is just as important as problem-solving. There are a lot of problems that are easy to solve once they are found and defined. Until then they give rise to a general disquiet and unease that cannot be tackled.

Tasks The definition of tasks and objectives. This may include the solving of problems but it can also include plans, decisions and areas of attention.

Activity Focusing on areas of activity which exist and also on new areas of activity and involvement. There may be more than enough activity already, but it may all be of the reactive type where someone else pulls the strings for the puppet to dance.

Balance Focusing on balance situations and seeing whether a balance is being achieved. Is there too much inward looking and not enough outward looking?

Priorities Focusing upon and setting up priorities. Are the priorities very clear or is there (usually) just a general impression with a feeling that they would be sorted out if a real need arose? Priorities need to be definite and not just an *ad hoc* reaction to a situation.

Conflict Defining areas of friction and conflict, especially as regards other people.

Focus is, of course, the tool that is used to explore an audit. The purpose of the audit is to make clear the status quo but also to offer an opportunity for improvement – towards happiness. It must be repeated that focus is much more difficult than it seems, and a deliberate effort must be made. The temptation is to deal in too general an area: for example, 'how could I be happier?'

4 Self-space examination

This is a specific type of audit which focuses directly on the self-space. What is included in the self-space? Which things can be done with ease, enjoyment and comfort? Does the self-space include *dependence* on outside things and other people? If so, these must be excluded from the self-space. It may be that the true self-space is very much smaller than at first imagined. The different self-spaces for different areas (work, family, etc.) can be examined. The self-space includes all those aspects of the life-space which can be *coped with* easily and with enjoyment. It may become obvious that the self-space is very small. This would indicate the need to inject activities which could serve to enlarge the self-space by providing things which could be done with ease and enjoyment. It is important to be ruthlessly honest about the self-space. If something can only be coped with when one is at the top of one's form then this must not be included. The self-space only includes those things which one can deal with *easily*. It is true that the self-space

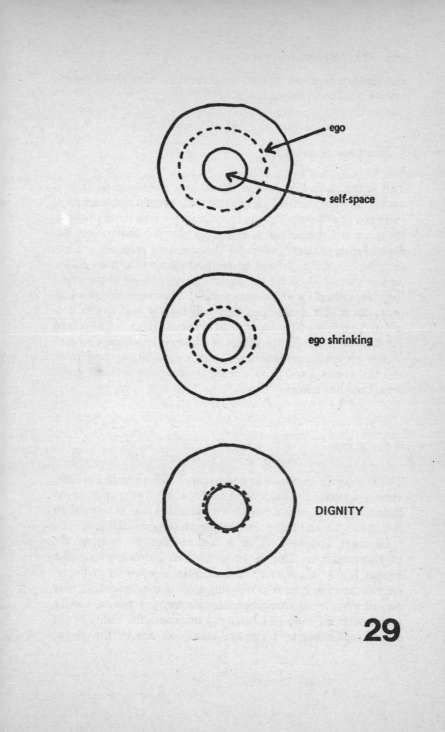

ego

self-space

ego shrinking

DIGNITY

29

can fluctuate from day to day, but a ruthless examination directs attention at the *minimum* space.

5 Life-space examination

This is the audit that focuses directly on the life-space. It is a matter of picking out – with honesty – the specific problems, pressures and expectations that go to make up the total *demand* of the life-space. It is important to remember that the life-space is the demand-space or operating-space. The problems, pressures and expectations should be defined as specific demands *first*. It may later become useful to look for the general source of some of the problems (for example a demanding family). The important point to remember is that specific problems will usually need specific solutions. Specific conflicts and sources of friction must also be picked out. General trends for the future and historic trends are also part of this life-space examination. Personal expectations, ambitions and the demands set upon oneself by temperament and greed should not be omitted.

6 Shrinking

This is a specific *operation* or endeavour. It follows from a general audit or a specific examination of the life-space. The purpose of the shrinking is *to increase happiness*. Shrinking can be applied in two specific areas: life-space shrinking and ego shrinking.

Life-space shrinking This is an attempt to increase the cope/demand ratio. This has been discussed in detail in an earlier section. It may be a matter of reducing the life-space by giving up some of the expectations or rejecting some of the demands. It may also be a matter of changing circumstances and solving specific problems. It may also be a matter of increasing the ability of the self to cope either by perceptual change or else by the 'shrug' process which cuts off over-reaction. Tolerance can also increase the ability to cope. Life-space shrinking is a matter of focusing on small specific areas and setting up definite tasks. It is a mistake to try to tackle too much at once.

Ego shrinking In previous sections 'dignity' has been defined as the coincidence of the ego, and the self-space as shown in Figure 29. Ego shrinking means cutting back the ego until it coincides with the self-space. This can only follow after an honest examination of the self-space. The purpose of the exercise is to reduce the demands and expectations that inevitably arise from an inflated ego. Until dignity has been achieved most people are *bullied by their egos*.

7 Expanding

This is another specific *operation* or endeavour. The purpose is to expand the self-space and with it to expand the areas and opportunities for happiness. It may involve an improvement in the ability to solve problems or cope with the pressures in the life-space. It may involve an improvement in thinking in general and lateral thinking for perceptual change in particular. It may involve cultivating the 'shrug' as a way of coping with over-reaction and conflict. It may involve reducing dependence on others, the approval of others and outside circumstances: that is to say, increasing self-reliance. The most direct way is to inject activities with which the self can cope easily and with enjoyment. This at least provides an area where one aspect of the self can be enlarged as well as increasing the overall cope/demand ratio.

Coping Increasing the ability to cope with the demands of the life-space either in terms of tackling specific problems and pressures, or by building up the general ability of the self to tackle these.

Activity Injecting activities which can be tackled with ease and enjoyment or expanding such activities if they already exist. As far as possible, involvement with the outside world should be included as part of these activities: for example, helping others or the use of organizing talents.

8 Practice and training

This is not unlike the training of Buddhism in general or Yoga or Zen or the training involved in sport. There may have to be an effort to practise things until they become easy and enjoyable. For some matters there is no magic switch or formula which can be applied to bring about an instant effect. The problem is that unless the effect follows immediately people get discouraged and give up. As with cleaning one's teeth, practice and training need to become a routine. We can look at some of the specific areas where training will be necessary and where it can make a difference.

Being positive People who have a naturally negative or pessimistic nature may have to make deliberate efforts to develop a positive attitude. Such people may have to make an effort to look for the positive aspects of a situation even though the many negative aspects appear to them first. It may be a matter of stopping oneself from saying something negative. Much of this practice arises in situations that involve other people. On one's own one can deliberately practise trying to look at problems and pressures as *opportunities*.

The shrug Avoiding being bullied by circumstances or enslaved by one's over-reactions. The separation of sensitivity from reaction. Assessing whether something is really important or threatening before reacting. It is a matter of practising the cutting off of reactions by a mental 'shrug'. This will have to be practised very deliberately before it becomes effective. In time someone who has had pleasure in upsetting you will find that he cannot any more.

Awareness activity This includes practice in sensitivity and awareness. It means practice in being able to look at the moment and to enjoy it instead of just looking through the moment to what comes next. It is practice in now-care as opposed to future-care. From time to time a person should pause to extract the full flavour from the moment. This does require very deliberate effort but can quickly become rewarding. Too long a time should not, however, be spent on it. Intense awareness should not be practised for more than five minutes at a time – but heightened appreciation and general now-care can be exercised for much longer.

Decision and problem-solving Most people need practice in decision and problem-solving in order to develop the strategies and habits of mind that some people find difficult. It is no use waiting until the really big decision comes along. Quite often it is a matter of getting used to looking at priorities or concentrating on what one is prepared to give up. Some of the decision strategies mentioned in earlier sections can also be used. Practice can include making a number of small decisions confidently and tackling small problems. Sometimes these can be set up deliberately as a training course.

Thinking This area needs a lot of deliberate practice, mainly because there are so many misconceptions about it. Practice should not be of the intellectual sort nor should it involve puzzles and games-playing. It should not be difficult or frustrating because the main purpose of the practice is to build up confidence and enjoyment. There should be no fear of being wrong or an urge to be proved right. It is a matter of thinking of a matter for a while and then cutting off rather than cudgelling one's brains for a solution. There will need to be deliberate and specific practice in lateral thinking because this is by no means a natural process and success depends entirely on the confidence that comes from practice. For example, it is quite easy to practise the use of 'po' especially in random juxtapositions. Another practice area is that of exlectics. This can be practised on one's own or in an argument. Trying to turn a dialectic argument into an exlectic one is good practice. The organization outlined in the last part of this book can provide a suitable setting for thinking practice.

9 Understanding

This is a general understanding of the background and structure of the new meta-system. It is this general understanding that provides the support both for the mood and also for the framework. The understanding can be practical rather than intellectual. It does not have to be defended in polemical situations. But an understanding is valuable to the practical application of the principles. An understanding shows why something is worth aiming for even if the immediate application does not seem to produce immediate results. After all, it is the *structure* of the meta-system that provides the meta-system and makes it more than just a package of 'be-good' exhortations. A sufficient understanding of the meta-system can be got from reading and re-reading this book. It can also help to encourage the others in your life-space to read it as well. Those who require a more detailed understanding of the patterning nature of perception can read *The Mechanism of Mind*, but this is unnecessary for an understanding of the meta-system as such.

In day-to-day life the general principle should be followed (for example the three respects) rather than attempts to tackle each situation by reference to the structure of the meta-system. The structure is the soil from which grow the vegetables that can be used.

10 Organization

The 'Network' organization described in the last part of this book can provide a structure of communication and an area of opportunity for those who find that their own attitudes are similar to those of the new meta-system. The new meta-system is, however, based on individuals dealing with themselves and in pursuit of their own happiness. There is no need to depend on this or any other organization for this purpose.

The most difficult thing is to teach what is obvious – because it is so easy to learn that it makes no impression

Many of the principles described in the new meta-system will not seem new if we concentrate on those aspects of them that are similar to aspects of established principles. For example, the respect of the selves of others may seem like the usual admonitions against selfishness – but in the new meta-system this arises not from a denial of self but from an *increased* emphasis on self-love and self-centredness. In any case novelty is not important. What is important is effective happiness. It would be absurd to eschew valuable principles because they had something in common with established ones. For example, there is an overlap between proto-truth and hypothesis but there is an important difference for those who can see it. Lateral thinking is also quite different from creativity even though the aim is the same. Novelty is only of value if it draws attention to something that merits attention.

Many of the principles will seem obvious and they are all the better for that. I believe that matters such as these ought to be simple and direct. I believe that the intrigue of complexity and ambiguity is unnecessary even though it may offer a career to the interpreters of the hidden wisdom. There is a danger in simplicity and that is that a person may see only the surface and not feel the need to go beneath it to the implications that matter. This is a danger that must be accepted if communication rather than self-expression is the purpose of writing a book.

It is very difficult to teach things that are obvious because the mind takes them for granted and skims on to something more complicated which is presumed to be more valuable. Because we can understand something we often believe that we do in fact practise it. A lot of research into thinking habits shows that in this area the most obvious and easily understood principles are not in fact used – although everyone would claim to use them. Attention to the obvious, a focus on the obvious and a deliberate effort to *use* what is obvious can be effective.

In this section we shall look at five easy steps that can provide the transition stage into the new meta-system. The fact that they may be simple and obvious should not obscure either the difficulty of using them or the value of using them.

1 The positive mood

This is a focus on the positive in day-to-day life; in thinking, and in dealing with oneself, others and the world. There is a concentration of happiness and enjoyment. Life is to be enjoyed. There is an emphasis on the importance of oneself as the foundation for happiness: a man who is at ease with himself is at ease with the world. Happiness with the self is based on dignity. Relationships with oneself and with others are based on respect.

2 Improvement

A journey of a thousand miles starts with one small step – but in a definite direction. Each small step follows the previous one. It is better to do a very little in a definite and steady way than to attempt a great deal now and then and be disappointed by failure. Focus and being definite are important. Man is in control of the inner world created by perception. Small tasks can be set up and accomplished. Relaxation and the 'shrug' are as much a task as the more action-based ones. Achievement is not a destination but an enjoyment of performance. If every action is made enjoyable then enjoyment is easy to come by.

3 Dignity

The shrinking of the ego to fit the self-space and so give dignity is an important first step. The ego should shrink-wrap itself around the self-space just as a plastic shrink-wrap enfolds a supermarket item. The pressures of the self upon the self should be built up through confidence, not imposed as a mould. A person who is unhappy needs first to look at his ego.

4 Space-care

To begin with, self-space care and life-space care should be of the simplest sort. This includes simple life-space maps for different areas (family, work, etc.). The next step is the identification of some simple tasks. These can include the injection of a new activity as a means of enlarging the self-space. There may also be a trimming of expectations, the solving of a particular problem or the identification of an area for perceptual change (looking at something in a new way).

It is important that only one thing be tackled at a time. Problems that cannot be solved need not lead to despair. Such problems are put on one side as 'pet problems' and attended to now and again, while the person moves on to other matters.

5 Role-playing

Long-distance runners practise short bursts of speed. In time the addition together of these short bursts of speed adds up to a general improvement in speed over the long distance. Self-improvement is a heavy *burden* if it has to be maintained all the time. If it becomes a burden or a chore then it defeats its own purpose which, in the new meta-system, is to develop happiness. It may be better to play-act at being good for short bursts at a time and then relax back into one's greedy, over-reacting self. The play-acting can be enjoyed as play-acting. In time, as the play-acted role becomes easier it can be sustained for longer. And if it proves more enjoyable then it can become the permanent life-style. If it does not prove more enjoyable then a new role must be created. A person ought to be able to switch into the role of the 'biodic man' (from the biodic symbol) and switch out again when the going gets rough.

Summary

The new meta-system is based on the deliberate pursuit of happiness. The foundation of happiness is recognized as the importance of self and the achievement of dignity. Relationships are based on respect. Through perception man's mind creates the world in which he actually lives. He can improve this world through the processes of change and adjustment. His tool for doing this is thinking. Any way of looking at the world is a proto-truth which is believable and usable as long as it is understood that it can be improved or replaced. This gives rise to tolerance and the principle of humour. Above all, the attitude is positive.

Part Four
Network

The nature of a sieve is to be full of holes: that is how it fulfils its particular function

The relationship between the new meta-system and the Network organization described in this section has been mentioned earlier in this book. There is *no* necessary relationship. The relationship has been described as resembling that of a glass and water. The glass, and especially a particular glass, is only one way of drinking water. Water can be drunk from other vessels and without any vessel. The new meta-system is deliberately personal and can be used by an individual on his own without the need to belong to any organization whatsoever. The Network may offer an opportunity area for activity and achievement and especially *the practice of thinking*, but all this can be achieved elsewhere. Conversely the Network is open to people who have not heard of the new meta-system or who disagree with it.

What the new meta-system and the Network do have in common is that in both there is an emphasis on a positive and constructive attitude of mind – and on the importance of thinking.

Purpose and nature of the Network

Fundamentally the Network is 'a communication network of thinkers'. The purpose and value of setting up such a network can be considered under several headings.

Structure

There is a value in a structure. The quarrel between freedom and
structure is a false one. There are structures which restrict and
determine behaviour and others which liberate it. Communication
devices, like a telephone or the mail system, serve to liberate behaviour and make possible things that would be difficult otherwise. The communication structure of the Network is intended
to have the same effect. At the moment, outside of specialized
groups, people have to communicate with each other through the
mass media in the sense that the media take their material from
life and then publish it for the general reader. The choice of what
is interesting is the choice of what will interest most people and
sell most copies of a newspaper. In any case, the filtering by the
editorial staff is highly personal, no matter how honest. A communication network can allow people of like interests to explore
those interests with more attention than would ever be possible
through the mass media.

The importance of thinking

The Network is based on an acknowledgement of the importance
of thinking both for an individual and also for the society in
which he lives. The stage has already been passed when a *laissez-
faire* attitude would do. Someone is doing the thinking – and if
not, then runaway events are doing their own thinking. The purpose of the Network is to create its own world in which thinking
matters. The Network has no political aims or intentions because
thinking transcends such temporary alignments. The Network is
supposed to be an area where thinking *as such* is acknowledged as
important. It is necessary to contrast this emphasis on thinking
with the academic tradition which is based on knowledge and
scholarship rather than on thinking. It is necessary to contrast

intellectualism and description with the practical thinking required for decision and action.

Group and individual

Thinking can be pursued as a solitary exercise in the way it has always been pursued. There is room for solitary thinking within the Network as well as outside it. There is, however, an advantage in a communicating network because it increases the opportunities for thinking. It becomes possible to think about other people's problems. It becomes possible to exchange views and to pursue discussions. Many great thinkers have added to their lonely thinking a correspondence with other people on matters of interest. If thinking is always done in isolation there are not many things that can be thought about except problems related to work or hobbies or general philosophic problems. There are many active but under-used minds crying out for situations to think about. *Problem finders* are as important as problem solvers and if the two can be brought together there is a useful symbiosis.

Thinking as a craft

A communication network can allow thinking to develop into a hobby, or more accurately a *craft*. Thinking can change from being idle speculation and the racing of the mental engine into a skill that can be developed and practised and applied. Just as a carpenter develops a skill in bringing something about, so, through a network, a thinker can develop a skill in bringing something about. The Network offers an activity opportunity and an opportunity for achievement – not of the competitive sort, but the achievement of performance. As such the Network provides an immediate opportunity for the sort of activity suggested in the other parts of the book for enlargement of the self-space. In a world which requires furniture the craft of the furniture-maker can thrive. In the Network world of thinking the craft of thinking can thrive.

Tone

With thinking, tone is surprisingly important. Thinking can so easily become intellectual games, word-play, ego-boosting argument, puzzle-solving, mystical speculation and philosophical pagoda-building that some effort is needed to keep thinking on the practical level of day-to-day effectiveness. These other, specialized, types of thinking are by no means excluded and even within the Network can become areas of special interest for those who enjoy that special interest. The broad tone of the Network will be directed, however, towards practical effectiveness.

Academy and gymnasium

In some ways the Network will become a distributed gymnasium or practice area for thinking. In other ways it will become an academy of thinkers who aim at exploring the nature of thinking itself and also applying it to specific problem areas. As suggested later, within the Network there may be specific task forces which choose to direct their thinking towards a particular objective. There can be no guarantee as to the excellence of the thinking so directed – that will depend on the skill of the thinkers who become involved. At times the Network – or part of it – may function as a collective think-tank for the generation of new ideas and new concepts. In effect the communication Network creates a university of thinkers who have in common their interest in being part of the Network.

Qualifications

It is necessary to be very clear and definite about the qualifications of those who may wish to join the Network. It must be emphasized that the Network is not a system for intellectuals nor is it restricted to those who have an especially high IQ. *Motivation* is much more important than talent. We can look at the entry qualifications under several headings.

Motivation   The prime requirement is that the members of the Network should be interested in thinking *as such*. The interest in thinking and the enjoyment of thinking are what matters. Those who regard thinking purely as a competitive boost to their ego and those who seek in the Network a platform to show how much brighter they are than others are specifically excluded. Those who might regard the Network as an élitist enclave of brilliant people must realize that this is not the intention. Talent, brilliance and high IQ do not matter so long as there is a genuine interest in thinking. People who have never regarded themselves as bright or intellectual or academic but who are interested in the area of thinking are welcomed. There are many aspects of thinking at which they might well be better than the self-styled intellectuals. Broad, robust, practical thinking is even more important than intellectual game-playing. Thinking is not intelligence but the operating skill through which intelligence acts upon experience. It is interest in that operating skill and its application that matters. Within the Network there will be opportunity to practise and develop the skill in thinking. What matters initially is the motivation to do so. The Network is not a shop-window but a workshop.

Involvement   There may eventually be room for those who only want to be lightly involved, but in the initial stages an essential entry requirement is a determination to make the Network function. This degree of involvement and determination is related to the motivation but includes the ability to carry through matters which may be uninspiring but which are necessary. Dabblers and dilettantes will not be able to make the Network effective.

An investment of determination and effort is necessary. Those who make the investment will have it returned in the achievement of seeing the Network function. This involvement does not have to be at the level of self-consuming enthusiasm but at the calm level of wanting to do something effectively and well.

Positive attitude   The attitude of the Network is similar to that of the new meta-system in this respect. The attitude is positive and constructive. It is a matter of *wanting* to build upon things and to bring them about. The attitude is exactly opposite to the negative attitude of fault-finding, criticism, destruction, opposition, complaint and nit-picking. The need to be right all the time and the dependence of one's ego on being right are not wanted. Those who wish to exercise pet hobby-horses or prejudices should find another arena. The importance of this positive attitude cannot be stressed enough. Nor will it do to claim that destructive criticism is really constructive because it is honest. There can be perfectly honest negative attitudes, but they are still negative. A positive attitude can still pay the necessary attention to faults, deficiencies and limitations but does so in a different perspective. It is appreciated that this matter of attitude will create many problems. Many of those who will claim to have a positive attitude will in fact – through habit and training – be unable to operate in any other mode than the negative. People who are normally interested in thinking tend to be prickly and very ego-sensitive. They do regard their thinking as part of their egos and cannot brook being wrong. They are apt to regard their own ideas as unique and to treat as achievement any hole they can knock in the ideas of others. Quite often they are surprisingly hostile – if they cannot solve a problem then it is because the problem-setter has deliberately misled them. In spite of these problems it must be accepted that anyone who joins the Network does so on the condition that his attitude is going to be positive.

Tolerance   Tolerance, humility and a sense of humour come together to give another essential requirement. There will be different levels of talent and different points of view in the Network and a great degree of tolerance will be necessary. As suggested before, those who regard the Network as a platform from which to insist that others accept their ideas are specifically excluded. Tolerance includes not only the acceptance of other people and of their right to a point of view, but also an undertaking not to force demands and expectations on others. Quite often I get sent lengthy theses with a *demand* that I appreciate the genius involved. Now there may well be genius involved, though more often there is simply another way of describing something (usually the universe). It may be possible in the Network to arrange that some members – who so wish – can be involved in this business of reacting to the ideas of others. Tolerance does not mean that one has to accept every idea as valid. But it does mean that one accepts the right of others to think – and the possibility of errors in one's own thinking.

Plurality

A definite feature of the Network is the recognition that different people have different talents. Especially in the area of practical thinking there are many parts to play. The idea that there is one sort of perfectly intelligent, perfect thinker is nonsense. Some of the best logical analysts are quite incapable of assessing priorities or making decisions. Some of the best synthesizers are incapable of generating original ideas. It is not suggested that a person can only have talent in one direction. But what is suggested is that there is room – and need – for different talents. Those who write in (as suggested later) should make an effort to set down their own area of talent and enjoyment. This is important.

Some different roles and talent areas are suggested below. These are by no means exclusive. In many cases there is an overlap between areas.

Operating

The different areas of operating are suggested first.

Organizers   Those whose talent lies in organizing things – in a practical rather than a theoretical way. This must include the talent for running organizations, not just for designing them.

Information compilers   Those who are good at collecting and collating information. They know where to find information and they know how to keep it alive and accessible.

Detectives   Those who are good at following a trail, and at finding things out. Those who can be set a general direction and will then find their own way there.

Researchers   Those who are good at putting together information to expand upon an idea or to support it. Those who are good at doing experiments in the real world or in the world of already accumulated information.

Idea generators   Those who pride themselves on their ability to generate new ideas, new concepts and new hypotheses. Those who are interested in creativity and new ideas. This must be a general ability – not the intention to pursue one single new idea that may have arisen at some time in the past.

Synthesizers   Those who are good at putting together a mass of data and then boiling it down to what is important. Those who are good at bringing different things together and from the synthesis creating something new.

Reactors   Those who are good at reviewing and reacting to existing situations or to the ideas of others. This is indeed a critical role, but it involves the genuine appraisal role of criticism and not the destructive approach.

Explainers   Those who are good at taking a complicated situation and explaining it in a direct and simple way. This is not unlike the role of a science journalist. This task of clarification and simplification must not assume special intelligence on the part of the receiver.

Communicators   Those who are good at communicating with

others, either in a direct way (face to face) or through some other medium (for example, writing). There is an overlap here with the explainers but also a distinct ability to communicate something as distinct from explaining it. A good teacher is a good communicator.

Salesmen Those who are good at the very important process of creating interest in others. This is the ability to help other people see something in a new way. In its proper sense it is a way of enrolling the emotions of others through a change in their perceptions.

Group organizers Those who are good at the type of organization required for handling a local or a regional group. This must take into account the realities of human nature and fluctuating enthusiasm. It must include the determination to keep things going in addition to a sensitivity to the way things are going.

Diplomats Those who are especially good at getting on with people. Those who have a facility for dealing with people on a one-to-one basis. Those who can put across a point of view without offence.

Leaders Those who like taking responsibility and making decisions. Those who find leadership a natural role rather than an opportunity to exert a power they feel they need. This should be based on past experience of leadership qualities rather than the desire to suppose that one is a leader.

Effectors Those who are good at *making things happen*. This is the most important role of all. It includes activity, direction and determination and also the skill to overcome obstacles. It is a personality skill more than an intellectual one.

Thinking

We can now consider the 'thinking' skills as distinct from the 'operating' skills. As before, the list is not complete and there can be considerable overlap.

Logic The process of examining implications and the making of deductions. A method of extracting even more information from what is available. An examination of behaviour within a special, constructed universe.

Analysis Clarity of vision and focus. The examination of problems and situations in order to provide the detailed map that can be used as the basis for decision. The ability to look beneath 'lump' concepts and total situations. The examination of trends and interactions.

Criticism Matching a suggestion with the view of the world provided by experience. Looking for internal inconsistencies. Giving equal attention to the worth-while aspects as well as the faults. Treating faults not as a means of destroying the idea but as areas for further improvement. Most criticism is based on a personal and expected view of the world.

Description The ability to describe a situation or a process. The usual purpose of description is understanding, but pleasure is equally valid. The describer provides a means of putting into the internal world map something which previously had only existed in the external world. Academic skills tend to be of this sort.

Assessment This is rather broader than criticism. It involves relating one thing to another and taking account of priorities. Whereas criticism is usually related to an ideal view of the world, assessment is based on the perspective of an actual world. Assessment may also involve holding in mind a general level of performance, as in assessing examination papers.

Observation The ability to notice and note. It may be a matter of accumulating enough observations to generate a concept or it may be a matter of using observation to support a concept. It may be a matter of extracting what is obvious or something that only becomes obvious *after* someone has observed it. Observation is related to the awareness activity described earlier in this book. Observation does not have to be comprehensive like description.

Lateral thinking The ability to look at things in new ways and generate new ideas. This is not just a sensitivity to new ideas or an interest in them. It is the deliberate ability to generate new ideas to order. A person who has, in his life, had one or two good ideas is not necessarily a good lateral thinker.

System design Setting up and designing systems of organization. Being able to foresee how things will function. This ability must include an emphasis on simplicity, directness and effectiveness: over-complicated systems are not required. There must also be taken into account the actual circumstances under which the system will function. The perfect system that will not function because of something unsuitable in the environment is no system. System design does *not* necessarily include the ability to organize and put into operation the system designed.

Problem-finding A very important ability indeed. Many people are much better at solving problems than at finding them. Many inventors have an inventive talent but no idea what to invent or where to apply it. The ability to focus upon a problem or opportunity and to define it is extremely important – even if the problem-finder has no skill in solving the problem.

Problem-solving The ability to solve problems and to *enjoy* solving problems. The ability to look beyond the first solution for one that is simpler and more direct. The aesthetic ability to choose between an adequate solution and an effective solution. At the same time the ability to offer practical solutions and not just ideal ones which cannot be used.

Evaluation The ability to apply emotions and other value systems to an idea or to a problem-solution. Since emotions are the ultimate arbiter of whether something is worth-while, this evaluating function is important – even if it is based on prejudice. This ability must include the ability to give not only a personal evaluation but one that would coincide with the evaluation of most other people. In effect, a 'feeler' who is able to crystallize and communicate those feelings.

Decision The ability to make decisions and to give the reasons for them. This also includes the ability to set up a decision by looking at the background, the alternatives, the decision criteria and the consequences of a decision. There must, however, be a definite decision and not just a *description* of decision alternatives with no final choice.

Coping The complex ability to cope with a total situation rather than to choose only that part of it which is easy to deal with. This may involve acting on insufficient information, making guesses and even using provocative (or testing) action. It is a broad practical ability which is based on a sensitivity that may be absent in ordinary decision-making. The coper must be able to cope whatever the situation and not sit back until more information is available.

Initiative The ability to set up initiatives and new projects instead of just reacting to circumstances and the problems provided by circumstances. This may involve leadership and it may involve creativity. Initiative *must* include a measure of practical sensitivity. There is not much point in always starting grandiose projects which are doomed to failure. Entrepreneurial talents would fit in this bracket.

Operation The ability and skills necessary to put things into action. Obviously the opposite of description. It may include the ability to follow instructions accurately or to follow the spirit of the instructions but make adjustments to fit the circumstances. This is a broad, practical ability not unlike coping but involving more planning and initiative.

Construction The important ability to build things up, either from scratch or from something that is on-going. The ability to modify and improve and generally to make things better. This can be on an intellectual level or on a practical level. The constructor is motivated to bring something into being. This may involve new ideas or the skilled use of old ideas.

Activity

The activities of the Network will ultimately depend on the way it evolves and on the interests and desires of the members. There will also be special interest groups who use the communicating structure of the Network to bring together people with these special interests. The Network will embrace many different types of activity, just as there is room for many different types of talent. The suggestions made here are only by way of example. It is expected that the self-organizing nature of the Network will, in time, provide further types of activity within the broad framework.

Group and individual There are those who prefer to work as a group and others who prefer to work entirely on their own. The Network will provide an opportunity for either temperament. A group structure will not be forced on the loner. Groups may be physical groups which meet together periodically or communication groups who communicate freely with each other. Groups may have regular meetings, *ad hoc* meetings or just annual meetings. There is no need for members of a group to like each other or to treat each other as friends – respect and tolerance are all that is required. Individuals would communicate with the centre or with other individuals.

Exploration of thinking In one of its aspects the Network will function as a general academy for the exploration of thinking. This may involve observations, suggestions, ideas, collection of data, collation of information, hypotheses, experiment design, experimenting, discussion and the like. The orientation will be that of practical operation as much as scientific analysis. For example, the teaching of thinking as a skill in schools is a search for the most effective way of doing this – in practice. Theorizing will not by itself solve the problem. Anecdotes and observations are just as valuable as more rigorous experiment – especially as the Network will offer an opportunity for many observations to be put together.

Thinking practice An important activity will be the provision of opportunity for the practice of thinking. This will be as an end in itself: for the sheer enjoyment of thinking and to develop more skill. For example, there might be weekly meetings of a small group who work their way through the CoRT Thinking Programme. There could also be groups who meet together on a regular basis to practise and develop skill in lateral thinking. This has already happened in Australia. Thinking can be a sport, a hobby and a craft like any other. There is no reason why people should not meet together to enjoy thinking just as they might meet to play tennis. On an individual basis there might be the circulation of problems and the generation of problems. Individual special interest groups may set up their own newsletters or journals. The special advantage of a network of thinkers is that the *thinking* of the members can be turned directly towards thinking up specific activities: a sort of positive feed-back.

Problem-solving This also includes the important area of problem-finding. There may be specific problems from the world at large that need thinking about, even if solution is not easy. Some members may direct their energies towards problem-finding and then these problems can be used for problem-solving enjoyment by others. It will also be possible for members to inject their own problems to provide a problem-solving opportunity for those who wish to solve these problems. Problem-solving can be done on a group basis or on an individual basis.

Task forces These would be special groups set up to direct their thinking towards a specified area. These areas could vary in nature from political to environmental, from mechanical to philosophical. For example, one task force could look into the possibility of developing a new principle of air-lift other than the conventional aerofoil wing. Another task force might look into the problem of job-satisfaction. Yet another might look into methods of reducing bureaucratic costs. Another group might be devising games that can be played with just two playing pieces. Groups can choose their own tasks or take one provided by a problem-finding task force. Groups would also decide how to tackle the problem: by collecting information; by generating ideas; by scientific analysis; or just by discussion. A group would also be able to ask for expert help from others in the Network.

Think-tank It may prove possible to set up idea-generating think-tanks which would attempt to generate new ideas on demand. If the new ideas were in relation to a real industrial problem or had commercial potential, then the think-tank could operate on a fee basis. It must be emphasized, however, that this type of activity would have to prove itself. It would never be possible for the Network as such to endorse such activity.

Communication medium As suggested earlier, the Network would provide a special communication medium in this area of thinking. The specific means by which this was carried out would develop in the course of the evolution of the Network and might include journals, newsletters, correspondence, meetings, phone conferences, visits and the like.

Thinking strategies A considerable part of the effort would be directed towards devising more useful operating strategies for thinking in general. This is an area in which, outside of mathematics, the human race has made surprisingly little progress. In the West, we often pride ourselves that our thinking is *approaching* that of the ancient Greek philosophers, whereas it should have progressed much further.

Network operation and organization As suggested earlier, much thinking will need to be directed inwards towards the organization and operating of the Network itself. It must, however, be realized that there will be differences of opinion and conflicting suggestions, each of which would be effective in itself. In this area a great deal of tolerance will have to be shown. The effectiveness of the Network must take priority over the ego-involvement in a particular idea. Yet once it gets going the Network will be able to embrace under its communication umbrella a variety of activities and forms.

Principles

In the specific activities of the Network the same principles will apply. These can be summarized as follows.

Definite This includes a definite focus and aim rather than waffle and drift. A discussion purely for the enjoyment of discussion is perfectly acceptable as a definite aim. But waffle, drift and confusion should be avoided.

Effective The aim should be for something that is practical and effective. This includes crispness and directness. Grandiose philosophical speculations are only suitable for special interest groups. This also applies to intellectual word-games and peacock-like displays of virtuosity.

Tolerance In this field of thinking there will have to be an enormous amount of tolerance. Ego-involvement and jealousies will wreck any structure unless this is realized in advance.

Respect There is also a vital need for respect towards the contribution of others – whatever it may be. The respect is directed towards the effort and motivation of the thinker and should not depend on the quality of the contribution. It is up to a group to make the best use of its contributors and to arrange areas in which they can really contribute.

Organization

The Network will be self-organizing in structure. Just as it is supposed that molecules self-organize to create the chemical basis of life, so the motivation, interest, involvement and direct investment of effort of those who wish to be part of it will create the structure. For this to happen there has to be a simple communication framework within which the effort can achieve results. This simple framework is what is outlined in this part of the book.

Eventually the organization may take a cellular form with small groups forming cells that are in contact with each other and with a centre. Or there may be a regional or national type of organization with a more centripetal structure. There will be enough flexibility for the evolution of the organization to reach the stable form that best suits its purpose. The organization will not take the form of a club nor will it be democratic in the first phases. This is to avoid politicizing, polemics and power factions who may seek to take over the organization for their own ends. No one has to join the communication network if he does not wish to – and those who have joined can leave at any time. The most important requirement in a telephone or mail system is that it should function effectively in practice and not just on paper. Clearly, if it is to function at all, the network will have to take account of the interests and wishes of the members, but this can best be done on a synthesizing basis rather than by the clash of different factions. This follows the exlectic process mentioned earlier in the book rather than the dialectic process.

Within the overall framework there may be different groups, regions or countries which may evolve their own particular types of organization to suit their needs. It is expected that in the initial stages much of the thought of the members can be directed towards such ends. There are times when the type of organization is determined by the particular circumstances of the moment and the availability of particular people. There may well be false starts and dead-ends, as happens with any evolutionary process. That is where the positive and constructive attitude comes in. A determination to make something work, coupled with skill and motivation, will succeed.

The first stage is to direct the interest and the investment of effort of those who wish to be involved.

Problems

There are certain problems connected with any organization of this sort which can be recognized from the start. These problems will be exaggerated by the nature of thinking and the people likely to be interested in this area.

Lack of consideration When a person makes an inquiry or submits an idea for an opinion he usually fails to consider that at the receiving point what was for him a one-to-one communication may become something else as all the individual inquiries accumulate. Many research organizations spend a great deal of their budget on answering inquiries and giving out information. This is far more than the mere cost of postage. In the case of the Network there will be no central organization to meet these costs until the organization has come about as described later.

Crispness In the area of thinking there is a tendency to elaborate and qualify and re-qualify until the approach to perfection has produced a mass of material. Again there is too little consideration for the fact that someone who has to react to this information will have to absorb it first. Crispness, directness and simplicity will have to be encouraged if everyone is not to be bogged down.

Flavours   There will be those who will wish to use the organization for their own ends. These need not be sinister. For instance, one group may wish to give a mystical, contemplative flavour to the process of thinking. In itself there is no harm in this so long as it does not get taken as the overall attitude of the Network, which remains practical and down-to-earth. Some sort of central control will be required to maintain the tone and the guidelines.

Eccentrics   The borderline between an eccentric, a freak and a 'nutter' is entirely subjective. One man's freak is another man's genius. There is room for all within the Network so long as it is understood that no one has the right to *demand* the attention or involvement of others. In any communication device that may come to be used the editorial judgement of those involved in running the device must prevail in the end. As suggested before, the Network will quickly atrophy if it is seen to be the platform for a few egocentrics. Within discussion groups or in communication with those who have chosen to look at unusual ideas the most eccentric of ideas may be communicated. It should be possible to communicate such ideas more broadly in an abbreviated form. The borderline between originality, plausibility and arrogant nonsense is, unfortunately, always subjective. This problem will remain a difficult one.

Involvement   Many organizations and meta-systems have various forms of ritual and meetings to reinforce the sheer *involvement* of the members, especially when they are not taking an active part. It may prove necessary to develop specific rituals or routines to give substance to involvement. For example, members may from time to time be asked for their ideas on a matter – even if this means returning the request with a 'no ideas' response. That at least provides something definite.

Endorsement   At different times efforts will be made to suggest that the Network organization as a whole endorses some idea, line of action or political attitude because a local group somewhere pretends that it does so. Such endorsements would be unfair to the other members. Attempts to suggest such endorsements could lead to exclusion from the Network.

Contribution

The benefit which a member gets from the Network will be in direct proportion to the effort he invests. It is not like a club in which a member pays a subscription and then endeavours to get his money's worth. It is more like a hobby or craft where the rewards depend entirely on the effort put in. As explained earlier, the purpose of the Network is precisely to make 'thinking' into a hobby. If a member gives the Network the importance of a packet of cigarettes a week then this is the measure of the importance it will have for him. It is up to each person to decide upon the place the Network can play in his life. As an area of activity and achievement the Network can offer an opportunity for involvement outside one's own backyard. As with many other organizations, the Network can only be what the efforts of its members make it. The types of contribution can be considered under four heads – three of which apply to the setting up of the structure of the Network.

Spread The more people who are involved in the Network the more quickly will it reach the critical size that will allow it to become viable. This is a matter of letting other people know about the organization – either through this book or in any other way. This has an advantage in that explaining the purpose of the Network to others can make it clearer for oneself.

Organizing work There will always be a great deal of organizing work to be done in keeping the communication network running. Those who have an ability in this regard should be prepared to offer this as their contribution. An amount of thinking work will also be required.

Funds The only funds entering the organization will be those contributed directly by its members. Since the Network is intended as a communication network for the benefit of its members they must be prepared to set it up. It is true that in the long term benefits may accrue to society, but an organization of thinkers that is too ineffective to set itself up does not deserve to be taken seriously. The cost of administration will make it necessary for all members to contribute funds unless they are in a position to offer administrative help that happens to be required at the moment.

Thinking Once the Network is set up and active then the contribution of members will mainly be in the form of the thinking that is used in various activities of the Network. In short, the first problem set to members of the Network is to set up an effective communication network of which they can become members. This is as important a problem as any other.

Start

The Network will start functioning as an organization as soon as the membership has reached a critical size that will make it viable. This critical size is in terms of numbers and in terms of the funds made available. During this latent period it may not be possible to answer inquiries. This latent period may be taken to extend for two years from the first publication of this book in each country.

Those readers who are interested enough to want to help set up such a network are asked to indicate their degree of interest. All correspondence must be accompanied by a *stamped and self-addressed* envelope (this will remain a basic rule of the network) and should be addressed to 'Network', c/o CoRT, 11 Warkworth Street, Cambridge. Contributors will be kept informed of the evolution and development of the organization. It may well be that the idea will appeal to very few people.

Suggestions and results of applied thought are welcomed, but it will not be possible to reply to these individually: the cumulative effect will, however, influence the development of the organization. In short, there is an investment in an idea which will only come about if the investment is sufficient.

With reference to the list of talents and abilities covered in this

30

section, each member is expected to indicate his own area of talent and enjoyment.

Symbol

The symbol of the Network is shown in Figure 30. It has no mystical significance but is a working symbol.

Summary

The Network is a communication network set up for those who wish to become involved in thinking as an area of activity. The relationship with the new meta-system described in the first part of this book is not one of dependence: either can exist on its own. There may, however, be a useful symbiosis since the positive, constructive attitude is required in both.

FOR THE BEST IN PAPERBACKS, LOOK FOR THE 🐧

In every corner of the world, on every subject under the sun, Penguin represents quality and variety – the very best in publishing today.

For complete information about books available from Penguin – including Puffins, Penguin Classics and Arkana – and how to order them, write to us at the appropriate address below. Please note that for copyright reasons the selection of books varies from country to country.

In the United Kingdom: Please write to *Dept E.P., Penguin Books Ltd, Harmondsworth, Middlesex, UB7 0DA.*

If you have any difficulty in obtaining a title, please send your order with the correct money, plus ten per cent for postage and packaging, to *PO Box No 11, West Drayton, Middlesex*

In the United States: Please write to *Dept BA, Penguin, 299 Murray Hill Parkway, East Rutherford, New Jersey 07073*

In Canada: Please write to *Penguin Books Canada Ltd, 2801 John Street, Markham, Ontario L3R 1B4*

In Australia: Please write to the *Marketing Department, Penguin Books Australia Ltd, P.O. Box 257, Ringwood, Victoria 3134*

In New Zealand: Please write to the *Marketing Department, Penguin Books (NZ) Ltd, Private Bag, Takapuna, Auckland 9*

In India: Please write to *Penguin Overseas Ltd, 706 Eros Apartments, 56 Nehru Place, New Delhi, 110019*

In the Netherlands: Please write to *Penguin Books Netherlands B.V., Postbus 195, NL–1380AD Weesp*

In West Germany: Please write to *Penguin Books Ltd, Friedrichstrasse 10–12, D–6000 Frankfurt/Main 1*

In Spain: Please write to *Alhambra Longman S.A., Fernandez de la Hoz 9, E–28010 Madrid*

In Italy: Please write to *Penguin Italia s.r.l., Via Como 4, I-20096 Pioltello (Milano)*

In France: Please write to *Penguin Books Ltd, 39 Rue de Montmorency, F-75003 Paris*

In Japan: Please write to *Longman Penguin Japan Co Ltd, Yamaguchi Building, 2–12–9 Kanda Jimbocho, Chiyoda-Ku, Tokyo 101*

BY THE SAME AUTHOR

The Use of Lateral Thinking

This book is a textbook of creativity. It shows how the habit of lateral thinking can be encouraged, how new ideas can be generated. Edward de Bono has worked out special techniques for doing this, in groups or alone, and the result is a triumph of entertaining education.

Practical Thinking

How is it that in an argument both sides are always right? How is it that no one ever makes a mistake on purpose but that mistakes get made? These are some of the questions that Edward de Bono answers in this book. His theme is everyday thinking, how the mind actually works – not how philosophers think it should work.

The Mechanism of Mind

In this fascinating and provocative book Dr de Bono illustrates with simple analogies the mind's tendency to create and consolidate rigid patterns, to build myths, to polarize and divide, and then relates these mechanisms to the various modes of thinking – natural, logical, mathematical and lateral.

The Five-Day Course in Thinking

This book offers a series of simple but intriguing problems in thinking that require no special knowledge and no mathematics. The problems are designed to let the reader find out about his own personal style of thinking, its weaknesses and strengths, and the methods, latent in himself, that he never uses. Being right is not always important – an error can often lead to the right decision.

Also published

Po: Beyond Yes and No
Lateral Thinking for Management
Conflicts: A Better Way to Resolve Them
Children Solve Problems
Atlas of Management Thinking
Future Positive
Teaching Thinking
Six Thinking Hats

BY THE SAME AUTHOR

I Am Right – You Are Wrong

In this book Dr Edward de Bono puts forward a direct challenge to what he calls the rock logic of Western thinking. Rock logic is based on rigid categories, absolutes, argument and adversarial point scoring. Instead he proposes the water logic of perception. Drawing on our understanding of the brain as a self-organizing information system. Dr de Bono shows that perception is the key to more constructive thinking and the serious creativity of design.

Handbook for a Positive Revolution

Traditional revolutions define an enemy and seek to overthrow that enemy. When you have got rid of the bad things then all is supposed to turn out well. Yet there are many people who have always felt that negativity is not enough. These are the people who will welcome the Positive Revolution. Edward de Bono's challenging new book provides a practical framework for a serious revolution which has no enemies but seeks to make things better.

Edward de Bono's Masterthinker's Handbook

It is never enough just to want to think or to exhort someone to think. What are the steps? What has to be done? Avoiding error and winning argument is only a tiny part of thinking. The main enemies of thinking are confusion, inertia and not knowing what to do next. The 'Body' framework designed by Edward de Bono overcomes these problems.

Opportunities
A Handbook of Business Opportunity Search

'An opportunity is as real an ingredient in business as raw material, labour or finance – but it only exists when you can see it'

Everybody assumes that he or she is opportunity-conscious – but is frequently only conscious of the *need* to be opportunity-conscious. For often what looks like an opportunity isn't one after all.

Opportunities is a handbook which offers a total, systematic approach to opportunity-seeking at both corporate and executive levels. It is Edward de Bono's most significant contribution to business since he developed lateral thinking – and should have just as much impact. Remember: 'Just before it comes into existence every business is an opportunity that someone has seen.'